INTRODUCTION

Great ideas and exciting technologies abound that aim to create environmentally sustainable products and services, promising to improve the health of the planet. In fact, they've been around for years. But why haven't we had a slew of innovative products and services that realize the promise of sustainability? Why don't we have scores of environmentally friendly companies touting their long-term successes? Why haven't we reached the tipping point for a new and greener economy?

The answer begins with this lesson: good ideas and amazing technology, by themselves, are not enough. The key component to making green innovations lasting and impactful is to make them attractive to the market and profitable. To be successful, these *greenovations*, as we call them, have to be **financially and economically feasible** and **scalable**. Without these components, good ideas can't get beyond being just good intentions.

In *Greenovate!*, we at the Center for Innovation, Excellence and Leadership and the Hult International Business School have surveyed some of the best innovations that do, indeed, fulfill that promise, as well as others that appear to have the potential to. We've gathered stories and learned lessons about sustainability from the path-breaking efforts of leaders, companies, non-profit organizations and governments from around the world. These lessons have demonstrated that there are innovative ways to make money *and* make a difference — ways that help us maintain our idealism by also satisfying the need to make a living.

In short, building on real and successful innovations that are green *and* sustainable would create a tremendous positive impact on our lives and the life of the planet. Just imagine:

What if ...

... WE COULD FIND DOZENS OF NEW WAYS TO CREATE *ALTERNATIVE AND CLEAN SOURCES OF ENERGY*, THEREBY DRAMATICALLY DECREASING OUR USE OF EXPENSIVE AND POLLUTING FOSSIL FUELS?

In solar power, technological strides have made solar more practical in terms of cost and flexibility of use: *Energy Innovations' Sunflower* solar farms have dramatically lowered the price of solar electricity while *Nanosolar* and *Konarka* are developing new ways to create and apply solar cells. *eThekwini Municipality's* (City of Durban) landfill gas-to-electricity project demonstrated that developed world solutions for clean energy can be successfully adapted to developing world situations. While many think this is a domain of high tech, there are also many low tech examples: *Empower Playgrounds* is converting children's play into electricity for schools while the City of Paris and JCDecaux are collaborating to make bicycles a viable public transportation option for commuters within Paris.

... WE COULD *RECYCLE, RE-USE AND EFFICIENTLY DISPOSE OF SUBSTANCES LEFT OVER FROM TODAY'S MANUFACTURING PROCESSES*, TURNING WASTE INTO USEFUL MATERIALS AND FUELS THAT WOULD OTHERWISE BE DUMPED INTO THE WORLD'S EVER-EXPANDING LANDFILLS?

In the realm of recycling, *Patagonia*, and *Terracyle* have succeeded in drawing most or all of their raw materials from recycled materials and then selling them in very different markets: clothing and consumer packaging. *Greenbox* replaces disposable moving boxes with rentable easy-to-stack plastic boxes made with recycled materials. In Indonesia, *Don Bosco* has actually succeeded in "putting old wine into new bottles" by converting oil for cooking into fuel for buses. *Big Belly*'s automated, solar-powered urban trash compactors can improve the entire waste-disposal system in urban areas, making them more energy- and labor-efficient while reducing the space that trash occupies. (And below, we'll discuss *PFNC*'s transformation of shipping containers into housing.)

... WE REALLY LOOKED AT THE WAY WE USED POWER AND FOUND WAYS REDUCE THE HUGE AMOUNTS OF ENERGY WE LOSE BECAUSE OF INEFFICIENT SYSTEMS AND EVEN SIMPLE CARELESSNESS—WHAT IF WE FOUND NEW WAYS TO *USE LESS POWER AND BECOME MORE EFFICIENT?*

In the domain of energy used for airplanes, Canada's *Bombardier* entered into a partnership with manufacturers to find ways to reduce fuel consumption while *UPS* has found ways to conserve on fuel use as well as lower noise pollution by changing the way it lands its planes. While Tesla has begun to succeed in creating a market for all-electric vehicles, *Bosch* and *Better Place* have found complementary ways to maximize the energy and minimize costs associated with hybrid and electric vehicles. *BAE Systems* has made a real impact in extending hybrid technology to much larger vehicles, such as city buses. The *One Laptop per Child* initiative and the retailer *Tesco*, although involved in very different domains, have both made an effort to analyze supply chains and processes to reduce costs and decrease energy use everywhere possible in their respective industries.

... WE COULD *IMPROVE PROCESSES RELATED TO AGRICULTURE AND FOOD PRODUCTION,* MAKING MORE FOOD AVAILABLE, CULTIVATION MORE SUSTAINABLE, AND PROCESSES LESS WASTEFUL THAN EVER BEFORE?

Creating and enforcing high standards of agricultural production that help to sustain the rainforest's natural resources is the creative contribution of the *Rainforest Alliance. Ikea's Farmer Field Schools* take the long view of educating cotton farmers in India and Pakistan on how to use less expensive and less toxic methods of farming, thus preserving the base of its supply chain. *Netafim's* drip irrigation system makes remarkable savings of water while improving irrigation systems. US's *Dairyland Power* has pioneered methods to convert waste into energy for farming while *BP Energy India*'s innovative business model has made it possible to distribute a sustainable cooking method throughout rural parts of India.

... WE COULD APPLY *MORE INTELLIGENT SYSTEMS* TO CONSERVING ENERGY AND DEVELOPING ALTERNATIVE SOURCES OF POWER, MAKING HUGE SAVINGS ON EMISSIONS AND COSTS?

The possibilities of applying contemporary computer power and analytics to finding efficiencies we could never dream of before opens up many opportunities for conservation and creativity, from the scale of the individual to whole cities and countries. On the small scale level, *Cisco Energywise, Oberlin College, Garmin* and *Progressive Insurance* have found ways to provide data and feedback all the way back to individuals to inform them about how they use energy; this information is then used as a foundation for reducing energy consumption. On a much larger scale, the EU's *E-Street* program and Malta's *Smart Grid* project benefits from the vision of government leaders who enable and fund the wide variety of players who must collaborate cohesively to scale up green initiatives big enough to meet the huge problems posed by climate change.

... WE COULD CREATE MORE EFFICIENT AND ENVIRONMENTALLY FRIENDLY *CONSTRUCTION PROCESSES AND BUILDING MATERIALS*, THUS ATTACKING ONE OF THE LARGEST EMITTERS OF HARMFUL GREENHOUSE GASSES AND PHYSICAL WASTE?

Going from planning to construction, a variety of initiatives have already begun that could revolutionize the energy consumed and wasted through construction. *LEED* is a standards group whose certification process awards buildings and builders for environmentally friendly construction and finished structures. *Axion* has succeeded in reducing waste while simultaneously improving the performance of construction materials. Finally, the *Bank of America Tower* reflected a decision of B of A to set green standards for a major high-rise building in the US by using the best technology to reduce its carbon and waste footprint while simultaneously making improvements to the building's operations.

... WE COULD SPREAD THESE GREENOVATIONS TO DEVELOPING REGIONS WHERE WE CAN
IMPROVE THE WEALTH, HEALTH AND ENVIRONMENT FOR PEOPLE AT THE BOTTOM OF THE PYRAMID?

Many examples mentioned above (e.g., *PFNC* and *One Laptop per Child*) also fit into this category. Some other notable instances follow the lead of initiatives such as *Empower Playgrounds* by finding ways to improve resource distribution without having to make huge investments in new infrastructure. *Grameen Danone*, for example, tends to the problem of hunger in Bangladesh by constructing eco-friendly yogurt mini-factories that will be located throughout the country, thus producing jobs and providing nourishment for surrounding villages. *Bloom Energy* uses the same logic of decentralization in its creation of large fuel cells that can power entire households located far away from conventional electric grids. In Nigeria, *Olam*'s business model innovation aims at aligning the interests of private capital, public institutions, and small farmers to create a revolutionary new market system to increase the quality and quantity of the production of a key staple, rice, while also adding significant gains to the income of farmers.

Defining Greenovations

We started our journey by defining "sustainable, green innovations" (or "greenovations") because, as with "innovation," we found the goal of making products and services "sustainable" to be a concept that is widely used, but often misunderstood. For our definition of greenovations, we combined our description of business innovation with a synthesized concept of sustainability as articulated by a number of leading global organizations:

> *Greenovations create and capture new value by meeting the needs of the present without compromising the ability of future generations to meet their needs.*

With this definition in hand, we have conducted extensive research on all types of businesses, initiatives, projects and technologies to identify the best examples of truly sustainable, green innovations — concepts that make money and improve the environmental equation.

Our Contribution to the Literature

One important characteristic that connects all these categories of innovation together, as well as the specific companies and organizations that are featured in these cases, is that these stories are about greenovations *in the here and now*. In contrast, there are many books that have made compelling arguments about how to link the markets and environmentalism *in the future*. Paul Hawken's *Natural Capitalism*, for example, made a splash by positing that of all the capital existing in the world, "natural capital" is the most undervalued. Governments could address this imbalance with a combination of incentives for good environmental behavior and taxes for bad. Although we heartily applaud his contention that natural capital makes "life possible and worth living on this planet," waiting for governments to become the prime impetus to push this kind of change in attitude may take longer than the planet can itself sustain.

For those of us more impatient to see business in sync with the needs of the environment, these examples of greenovations demonstrate that we don't have to wait for huge changes in the world's laws or in political movements or philosophy to make the planet greener and make money while doing it. In other words, one message underneath these stories is that it's time to stop debating about whether we can or should make money off greenovations; instead, it's time to get busy. Our innovative and compact method of getting the most important elements of business cases in a page or two — building off our earlier work in *101 Breakthrough Innovations* — was created with the intention of sharing the core lessons of these innovations (individually and collectively) as efficiently as possible with the hope of spurring people to move from theory to practice.

In many ways, **Greenovate!** amplifies the message of Daniel Esty's influential *Green to Gold*, which offers a very useful argument to business executives on how to green their businesses by integrating environmentally beneficial processes and products into their strategy. Strategy always comes first, Esty reminds us, because it blazes the path to sustaining profits. Green turns to gold when environmentalism is folded into that strategy. We wholeheartedly agree that all businesses cannot forget profit, no matter how philanthropic some of their goals may be.

In *Greenovate!*, we open Esty's lens on profitable green businesses geographically and economically, including many businesses and organizations of varying sizes from all over the globe. We also devote some attention to businesses whose goal is to transform the lives of people at the bottom of the economic pyramid — Grameen Danone in Bangladesh being one of the most striking instances. In examples such as these, we implicitly agree with Jack Hollander's main argument in *The Real Environmental Crisis*, which critiques the implicit contradiction held by many people between environmental goals and making money. Far from contradictory, it is affluent societies, he argues, that have the luxury to devote resources to environmental preservation and conservation. The US's Endangered Species Act is a prime example of an initiative that would find little support in impoverished countries whose populations are focused mainly on their own survival — unless, as has been demonstrated by many countries, such programs are integrated into tourism and sustainable development programs.

Many disagreeing with Hollander would contend that making money in a capitalistic system is inherently un-environmental because capitalism's need to grow continually can not be sustained. But, *Greenovate!* suggests that if capitalistic businesses grow from a foundation of sustainable practices, then capitalism's drain on limited resources can be limited — as long as we're innovating in a green way.

Pulling Rather than Pushing Greenovations on to the Fast Track

Despite our excitement over the many lessons of this book, we realize that that ultimate goal of creating a greener economy will not be achieved overnight. A series of small and large advances on many fronts will be required. Of course, social responsibility can and will play a role in the world's progress, but we cannot rely on this as a way to achieve our goals. Instead, we should build upon it.

Indeed, combining environmental consciousness with innovative business practices may be the surprise leading edge of the movement to save the planet in the twenty-first century. Thanks to the kind of growing popular pressure Esty points to as a driver for change (seen in changing consumer preferences as well as in government incentives and regulations), companies, economies and societies around the world are eagerly looking for capabilities to use all resources more efficiently.

But innovating in the here and now to make our methods of production and consumption greener and more sustainable requires making fundamental changes in a very complicated world created by decades of environmentally unsustainable economic structures. Because of those complications, we have to find more ways to pull (through demand) rather than push (through mandates or the simple offering of new technologies) greener habits and processes through the market with the explicit and tacit cooperation of the majority of the world's population.

Although we need revolutionary, comprehensive economic change to save the planet, we have to realize the promise of that revolution through evolutionary adoption processes. In other words, we have to make the necessary changes in behavior, cultures and economies easy rather than hard. As innovation advisors and teachers to hundreds of companies over the past thirty-five years, we have encountered two major barriers to addressing most of the environmental challenges the world faces.

FIRSTLY, A GREEN ECONOMY MUST BE BUILT UPON INNOVATIONS THAT ARE FINANCIALLY SUSTAINABLE.

As we mentioned above, idealists have often seen an inherent tension between making money and doing good. We would contend that making money employs and sustains people; hence, it motivates people to create and promote particular products and services. Although many corporations and people around the world aspire to support high ideals for tomorrow, most have to make money today to survive. What we advocate is using innovation to eliminate this false tension between profit and idealism. Building on significant innovation in both products and services as well as in processes and business models to create greener businesses, we hope that we can also create a significant innovation in economic outlook—one that sees a future that is both prosperous and green. For while it is certainly true that there is no future without a present, it is also true that there is not much of a present without the promise of a future.

As we at Hult International Business School and at the Center for Innovation, Excellence and Leadership have worked in this area, it has become evident that there are many books on green and sustainable business practices and many more on innovation. However, there are not many that bring these two together with a focus on gathering information about the areas where innovation meets environmental sustainability to uncover the true root causes and critical lessons that enabled these strides forward.

SECONDLY, INFORMATION ABOUT GREEN BUSINESS PRACTICES HAS TO BE GATHERED AND THEN WIDELY DISTRIBUTED.

We believe that problems of global scale must be addressed with global resources, experiences, and knowledge. In our research we have found inspiring stories of sustainable business innovations from all directions — cases from Canada to Brazil as well as from Finland to Ghana.

While these cases have often documented the wonderful regional impacts of green innovation, their potential to change the world is limited if information about them does not go beyond their region of origin. In publishing *Greenovate!*, we've tried to scan the world for some of the most notable efforts linking innovation and environmental sustainability. We hope they can provide examples, instruction and inspiration for your own future contributions to a green world economy.

In short, this book strives to provide stories of how many of the world's leading and emerging companies are addressing sustainability issues with profitable solutions that can spur even more innovation, growth and development as individuals and companies realize that being green does not mean being in the red. While there are a wide variety of approaches to this challenge, there are also common threads connecting many of the cases to one another, as in the categories of greenovations answering the question, "What If?" in the opening of this book. Moreover, there are some common themes running through all the cases that should offer insights to all those wanting to pursue sustainability solutions.

Insights for Driving Sustainability Innovations

The first set of insights relates to the ways in which organizations have been most successful in creating sustainability innovations and getting them to market:

PATIENCE AND TIMING

Sustainability innovations often require new-to-the-world technologies and/or significant changes in behavior from consumers. Neither of these can be easily achieved in the short-term. Companies that are focused and organized for the long march often manage to win—see Toyota's commitment to hybrids that can achieve 100% improvements in gas efficiency versus marginal improvements in the existing combustion engine. By not pacifying the near-term needs of stakeholders, the companies in this book have avoided falling in the trap of "greenwashing" and have actually captured the inherent opportunity in achieving sustainability. But patience is often not enough. Timing also counts, for being too early or too late to the market can mean, in the first instance, offering a product nobody is interested in or, in the second, entering an market that no longer has room for your innovation.

PASSION AND PERSISTENCE

To support the long march for the big win, we found that company leaders were both excited and personally motivated to build and drive the business. Whether it was to change the world and make it a better place (*Oberlin College* or *Grameen Danone*) or to make a lot of money (Konarka), the passion and persistence of these leaders were crucial in overcoming daunting challenges: from bringing new technologies to the market to changing consumer/customer behaviors to implementing different business models. It is clear that sustainable greenovations cannot be left to managers but require leaders whose passion and persistence provide the energy and stamina to overcome the range of barriers that will arise.

CREATIVE BUSINESS MODELS

There is a virtuous cycle in making something that is valued by the market and doing it profitably. We find that sustainability offerings that have a clear value proposition to the consumer/customer combined with a profitable business model have greater market acceptance and higher growth rates. As an example, *Zipcar's* new business model is offering drivers an alternative to owning a car or even renting a car. Offering a subscription model of car use that gives the company a base of steady cash flow, *Zipcar* also relieves infrequent or sporadic car users of the burden of paying for gas, insurance, and maintenance as well as the sheer cost of buying a car. People interested in occasionally renting a car can find that Zipcars are conveniently dispersed throughout dense urban locations. Automation allows riders access to codes that unlock the cars. The company is also open to innovative partnerships with large institutions that can support a fleet of cars, such as a municipality or a university. Enabled by the insightful application of automation, Zipcar is searching out various ways to monetize its new offering.

Insights for Making Sustainability Innovations Last

The second set of insights we uncovered is that almost all of the green innovations we analyzed achieve more sustainable outcomes because the companies and organizations that promoted these innovations found ways to maximize their efforts or minimize their costs in ways that consistently found success in the market. This was accomplished through using one or more of the four methods summarized below:

DO MORE WITH LESS

By focusing on improving the efficiency of resource use, these offerings will extend the ability to use the finite amount of non-renewable resources. These incremental innovations are critical as they act as a bridge to technologies that can take full advantage of renewable resources that are either too new or too costly to act as substitutes for non-renewable resources in the immediate future. Furthermore, when our economies are finally able to run on renewable resources, our systems and infrastructure will sip rather than guzzle, lowering the level of investment required to introduce more greenovations in the future.

For example, as the world's first mass-produced hybrid vehicle, the *Toyota Prius* achieves incredible gas mileage with a car that works with the existing transportation system. Although both Toyota and other car companies started work on alternative fuel vehicles at roughly the same time, many of the others have tried to bite off more than the market can chew: their overly-ambitious 100% electric cars needed many more billions of dollars and more development years *in addition* to the added requirements of creating new infrastructure and changing customer behavior. And while the other car companies have quickly rolled out hybrid options in the past few years, Toyota has already built a dominant position: the company released its third generation hybrid system this year (despite its recent recall problems which should prove to be a temporary bump rather than a permanent obstacle).

SUBSTITUTE WITHOUT SACRIFICING PERFORMANCE

These products and technologies replace scarce or finite resources with more widely available or renewable ones: organic plastic instead of petrol-based plastic or bamboo instead of wood. These innovations also include fully recyclable and upcycled products. As we mentioned earlier, *Greenbox* makes plastic moving boxes and other equipment from recycled materials, and, in the ultimate move towards sustainability, recycles its worn-out equipment into new boxes.

INFORM AND EMPOWER

These solutions provide people with accurate, relevant information on how, when and why resources are being used. Armed with this information, users are changing their behavior in significant ways. These types of innovations are critical: while technology will drive many of the sustainability gains, these benefits can be eclipsed by simple changes in human behavior. Providing detailed information on how community resources are used by individuals enables those individuals to self-monitor and adjust. Two projects in their early stages mentioned above — *Cisco's Energywise* and *Oberlin College's Energy Use Feedback System* — have demonstrated that as information on resource use is made more granular, individuals make better and smarter decisions. And both initiatives are working to lower implementation costs and increase the return on investment via lower operating costs for homes, offices and other buildings.

FIND THE WIN-WIN-WIN

This final case includes sustainable green innovations that align the incentives of many to achieve sustainable outcomes. These examples usually involve at least three different groups, each with very different needs, resources and behaviors. For example, *PFNC* takes empty shipping containers that are too expensive to recycle or ship empty back to China and converts them into affordable, stackable homes for Mexican workers. These workers living directly across the US border were typically housed in cardboard and aluminum shantytowns. Although these basic structures, outfitted with renewable or recyclable materials, cost less than $8,000 to create, the houses remained too expensive for the workers. However, PFNC is working with the large US corporations that employ these low-income laborers to pay the upfront housing cost to PFNC and then deduct a manageable amount from each employee each month. The US firms like the idea because it creates sturdy homes and stable communities that lower the high attrition rates typical of these workers. PFNC makes enough money to continue upcycling shipping containers costs and to invest for future growth. And the Mexican workers get affordable, developed-world housing.

Who Belongs in *"Greenovate!"* — now and in the future?

In gathering cases for this book, we chose the innovations that were creating the most buzz *and* seemed to have the most potential for long-term success. Their ability to capture value makes them truly sustainable — either as innovations attached to a particular company or innovations that could be spread throughout an industry or even a whole economy. We also chose companies that had a good deal of information in the public domain, which left out very many interesting stories in places like Japan and Korea.

But we don't see this book as an end in itself; instead, we see it as a way to inspire more efforts to greenovate and more efforts to gather and share information. To that end, we are doing two things to continue the momentum of *Greenovate!*. Firstly, this book marks the beginning of the *Beyond Eureka!* series of books highlighting innovations that are leading the way across a range of themes (not just stainability). Secondly, this book will be followed by an IXL *Greenovate!* web site, where we hope to continue the conversation on the connection between innovation and green business practices. In turn, that conversation can become a library for leading-edge information on innovation that companies draw from. Some of these innovations and companies are speculative and we are optimistic that they will succeed; however, we do also recognize that we take the risk that we might be wrong about their future. In those cases, we have a plan to replace these unsuccessful innovations in the next version of *Greenovate!*

If we've overlooked your organization's greenovation, we invite you to add your voice by posting your company's accomplishments and goals in this space. We very much look forward to hearing from you.

For more information, please visit http://greenovate.ixl-center.com

HOW TO READ THIS BOOK

In addition to the categorization of greenovations in the opening pages, it may also be helpful to provide a description of the discursive elements of the cases that have enabled us to condense these stories into a format that is both informative and concise.

The story of each greenovation is captured on two pages. The first page provides a concise overview by answering three questions: What is the innovation? Why is it sustainable? What has the result been? The second page chronicles in greater detail the Drivers, Barriers, and Enablers for the innovation; or, in other words, how did the innovation come about? In addition, the Impact on internal and external stakeholders is described. At the end, we look over the horizon to ask "What's Next?" for the organization and/or the innovation.

In the spirit of innovation, we've added a unique layer of information to the second page of the cases. The reader will notice that the content in the vast majority of cases is organized graphically in rows (described in the preceding paragraph) *and* in columns. In other words, in addition to reading the cases left to right, many stories can be read in columns from top to bottom. In the case of Bombardier, for example, the left column of the case deals with cost cutting, the middle with the persuading airlines to adopt new technology, and the right column with exploring innovative ways to find customers in tough economic times.

HOW TO USE THIS BOOK

1. **Convince your organization that you can do it, too.** Most if not all of these greenovations offer a story about overcoming obstacles to success—from solving technical problems to changing consumer habits. Calibrating the innovation to the economic context and the consumer need, greenovating organizations are making a difference in small villages in Peru as well as continental-size changes across Europe. They've done it, so you can, too.

2. **Generate ideas about how to innovate—whether around using less, creating new, or developing new business models.** With 50 examples from a wide range of organizations serving regions in many different stages of development, real material for brainstorming for new greenovations abound—either within the industry or market your organization already occupies, or in new spaces where opportunities are emerging.

3. **Buy something specific from these companies and organizations to help them become profitable and grow.** Money talks, and greenovations will flower faster and sooner with the financial backing of consumers. Because most of them offer cheaper and more efficient alternatives to traditional products and services, greenovations will also make a positive difference to the bottom line of consumers.

4. **Spread the word about greenovating.** Whether you refer others to this book, to the stories inside it, or just the insights they've helped to generate, you can help us move to a greener economy, changing hearts and minds one at a time around the world. If *Greenovate!* inspires you to green your own company or organization, keep the momentum going and share these stories with anybody you know who might be inspired, too.

All of us at the Center for Innovation, Excellence, and Leadership (IXL Center) hope that these stories enable you to think and act more innovatively as we all move to create a more sustainable economy and society.

Next-Gen Fuel Cell Technology

A cost-saving fuel cell technology that provides significant improvements in performance

INNOVATION
ACAL Energy developed a new method for generating current within a fuel cell by using a proprietary recirculating liquid cathode technology that performs better and at lower cost than existing fuel cell systems

SUSTAINABILITY
As with other fuel cell systems, the only by-products of the fuel cells are water and heat

In addition, ACAL's technology reduces the required amount of platinum, a rare and expensive mineral

RESULTS
The new technology enables fuel cell systems to operate up to five times longer than is currently possible

ACAL Energy cuts the amount of platinum used in fuel cells by 80% and reduces the price of fuel cells by 40%

DRIVERS

TECHNOLOGY PUSH: Fuel cells are unique in energy delivery, combining benefits such as: low or zero emissions, high efficiency and reliability, multi-fuel capability, no noise pollution

FOUNDER'S EXPERTISE: Dr Andrew Creeth, the founder of ACAL Energy Ltd with more than 15 years scientific experience, invented a new technology for ACAL

DEMAND PULL: According to Clean Edge, the fuel cell market is expected to grow steadily to $15.6 billion over the next decade — about 10x its 2008 size

GOVERNMENT PUSH: To cut carbon emissions, UK government sets up organization and business incubators to support start-ups and emerging technologies

BARRIERS

PRECIOUS METAL: Fuel cells require the use of precious metals (usually platinum) as catalysts — the scarcity and expense of these metals make the fuel cells unaffordable for mass use

BUSINESS RESOURCES: The company needed funds in order to take the technology forward from small-scale laboratory systems to manufacturable prototypes

COMPLEX EQUIPMENT: Sophisticated components and systems are required to ensure fuel cell reliability contributing to the high cost of current systems

BUILDING TRUST: FlowCath™ technology is new on the market and the lack of brand recognition is a challenge to attracting customers

ENABLERS

CHEAP ALTERNATIVE: Acal's FlowCath™ technology removes the need for platinum, replacing it with a proprietary liquid that is continuously pumped through the cell

CRITICAL INVESTORS: The company is supported by UK VCs, Japanese and European corporations, and public investors — altogether, they provided £7 million in funding

SIMPLIFICATION: The use of liquid instead of platinum allows simplification of equipment, thus eliminating the need for a hydration system

COMMITTED PARTNER: Carbon Trust, a UK government organization, assesses and supports the development of FlowCath™, increasing its credibility

IMPACT

COST REDUCTION: FlowCath™ allows an 80% reduction of platinum used in fuel cells and a 40% decrease in fuel cell price

INTERNAL: ACAL Energy built a state-of-the-art lab and a 4,000 m^2 plant, growing from 5 to 23 employees in 18 months

PERFORMANCE: The use of the liquid improves the fuel cell's durability to more than 1,500 hours with no loss in performance

AWARD WINNER: ACAL Energy was a finalist in 2009 Carbon Trust Innovation Awards, which recognize innovative, low-carbon companies

WHAT'S NEXT?

The company's near term strategy is to build partnerships with key supply chain companies and fuel cell OEMs. In the long term it plans to enter more markets: transportation as well as industrial and domestic distributed energy.

Kindle Wireless eReading Platform

Eliminate traditional print waste and costs through eContent, available anytime, anywhere through a simple eReader that is customized for you

INNOVATION
Kindle combines new wireless and eInk display technologies

Amazon provides a critical mass of titles

Purchase process is painless and computer-free

SUSTAINABILITY
Beyond saving trees, digital content eliminates pollution and waste from papermaking, printing, transportation and storage

eInk technology is very energy efficient, consuming zero energy in steady-state

IMPACT
The annual energy required to read a newspaper on a Kindle (including device production, data transmitting and energy use) is estimated to be 90% less than that used for a print copy or a newspaper

DRIVERS

TACKLE THE ELEPHANT: Print media consumes over 160 million trees per year in the US — even small reductions by stakeholders conserves significant resources

BIG BOLD STATEMENT: One aspect of Amazon's core mission is to provide "any book, anywhere at any time" — the Kindle brings this goal one step closer to reality

BURNING PLATFORM: Decline of print media has forced writers, publishers, and booksellers to find new ways to remain viable with electronic media

BARRIERS

SACRIFICE NOTHING: The target market — prolific readers — is often purists for whom the feel of traditional reading is a minimum requirement

WHOSE IP IS IT?: As with digital music and video, it is very difficult to deal with intellectual property protection of digital print — authors and publishers are skeptical

CHICKEN OR THE EGG: eReaders took off slowly as customers wanted lots of content before purchasing and publishers wanted a big e-market before going digital

NO UNIVERSAL STANDARDS: A common, easily readable and transferable format of the e-books was not available to users who avoid new technologies

ENABLERS

SKUNKWORKS: Amazon created a subsidiary to develop a device that was closer to an enhanced book than a digital device that displayed text

IMPROVING TECHNOLOGY: The project was further supported by advances in wireless connectivity and eInk display, which allowed reading digital texts without a computer

SCALE EFFECTS: Amazon's size and influence in print media enabled the company to bring customers and publishers together in a viable model for both, enabling cheaper overall prices while maintaining profitability

SENIOR SUPPORT: Amazon's Jeff Bezos has made the Kindle his pet project, ensuring strong organizational support and commitment to successful implementation

IMPACT

INTERNAL: By eliminating shipping and production costs, the profit margin for Amazon could be bigger than for paper books, providing new growth sources

COMPETITORS: Amazon has developed a proprietary system to support the Kindle (similar to Apple's iPod and iTunes), thus creating barriers to entry

INDUSTRY: The substantial growth and margins for the eBook industry will spur innovation and new entrants to challenge Amazon

ENVIRONMENT: With an estimated 1.2 million or more Kindles sold through 2009, digital reading could save thousands of acres of trees

WHAT'S NEXT?

The Kindle is bucking the trend to free, ad-supported content on the internet. If Amazon, other eReader manufacturers and content companies can build on this success, the print media industry could develop new, more environmentally and financially sustainable business models for the future.

Recycled Plastics as Building Materials

Transforming consumer and industrial plastics into eco-friendly construction materials that are strong as steel, longer lasting than wood, lightweight and cost competitive

INNOVATION
Proprietary formula for creating building materials from discarded plastics that are strong and will not rot, rust or corrode

Focus on specific lead customers (e.g., military, railroad ties) that need more cost-effective or better-performing alternatives than existing solutions

SUSTAINABILITY
Recycled consumer and industrial hard plastics destined for landfills are used to replace traditional construction materials such as wood, concrete and steel

RESULTS
Axion's construction materials have been used by the US army to build bridges that can support the weight of tanks in excess of 70 tons and require virtually no maintenance

DRIVERS

NOWHERE TO GO: In 1987, a barge carrying 3,100 tons of garbage was turned away by every landfill site on the US east coast, symbolizing the trash disposal crisis and spurring an increase in recycling activities

TIME AND COST: The US Army welcomed proposals for alternative solutions when they needed to replace an old wooden bridge in Fort Bragg but were discouraged by time requirements of using concrete or steel materials

REGULATORY PUSH: The EPA has worked with manufacturers to phase out chemically treated lumber due to environmental and health concerns, prompting the search for a replacement for wood preservatives

BARRIERS

LACK OF STANDARDS: The absence of performance-based specifications and procurement guidelines contributed to the lack of market adoption for recycled plastic lumber

HEAVY WEIGHTS: Axion won the Army RFP— while the first bridges they built with the plastic material demonstrated its ability to support cars and trucks, it had not yet proven able to support a 70-ton tank

UNPROVEN TECHNOLOGY: Currently, only 1%-3% of railroad crossties replaced each year are made from plastic composites because of the uncertainty whether plastic ties fare better than wood ties in long-term testing

ENABLERS

STANDARDS COMMITTEE: A committee of researchers, engineers and recycled plastic manufacturers worked cooperatively to develop test methods and standards that would guide the use of these materials

INNOVATIVE CONSTRUCTION: By bolting two T-beams together to form a new I-beam and using more pilings to support the new beams, Axion was able to build a bridge that can withstand heavier loads

TESTING: The plastic railroad ties produced by Axion were tested by the American Association of Railroads in Colorado to prove that its plastic ties last longer than wooden ties

IMPACT

INTERNAL: Axion has started receiving orders from major US and Canadian railroad companies for their railroad ties and a contract from the US Army to build more bridges

LONGER LIFECYLE: The resulting bridge is not only cheaper to construct, but it also costs less to maintain over a long period than wooden bridges that are often weakened by rot and insect damage

NEW MARKETS: Demand for blended plastics that can withstand high pressure has grown in commercial applications such as decking — this will introduce the product to the residential market

WHAT'S NEXT?

New ideas such as combining blended plastics with the I-beam decking system in residential building structures will make the system cost-competitive compared to traditional wood lumber and bio-composites.

HybriDrive® Propulsions Systems
Using hybrid system technologies developed for defense applications for large commercial vehicles to enable cleaner, smarter power for city buses

INNOVATION
BAE Systems' HybriDrive® hybrid electric drive system integrates engines, motors, generators, energy storage systems, and power control

Modular and fuel-cell ready

Commercial success story from a defense company

SUSTAINABILITY
Better fuel economy and lower emissions

Reduced maintenance and higher reliability

Quieter operation, smoother ride, and increased passenger comfort and satisfaction

RESULTS
More than 2,000 buses on the road, with more than 100 million miles of service

10 million gallons of fuel saved; 100,000 tons of carbon dioxide and 500 tons of nitrogen oxides prevented

DRIVERS

HIGH COST OF FUEL: For heavy vehicles in constant use, the cost of fuel is a significant contributor to operating costs

GOVERNMENT PUSH: Strict emissions rules for city buses and purchase subsidies encourage transit authorities to buy clean buses

INFRASTRUCTURE AVOIDANCE: Infrastructure-intensive compressed natural gas was the standard approach for meeting emissions regulations

PUBLIC IMAGE: Cleaner, quieter, more comfortable buses mean better transportation for all

BARRIERS

ADVANCED ENERGY STORAGE: Both lithium ion packs and fuel cell packs are still high cost and high weight

UNPROVEN TECHNOLOGY: The truck and bus industry is conservative and resistant to change, especially with respect to unproven technologies

SUPPLY BASE: System required high-power and high-energy-density components that previously were not available in the supply base

KNOWLEDGE BASE: Few companies had the breadth of knowledge, experience, and capabilities to make hybrid electric propulsion reliable

ENABLERS

SYSTEM INTEGRATION: Integrated, multi-disciplinary design capabilities enable hybrid electric components to work together

EARLY ADOPTERS: New York City led the way in demonstrating, developing, and maturing hybrid technology — it now operates the world's largest hybrid bus fleet

COMMITTED PARTNERS: Daimler Buses North America and the UK's Alexander Dennis Ltd. invested to incorporate hybrid electric technology into their platforms

SIMULATION SYSTEMS: Multi-level, multi-disciplinary simulation techniques enabled components and systems to be developed faster, shortening payback time

IMPACT

INTERNAL: These innovations have enabled BAE Systems to bridge the gap between military and civilian markets and technologies

URBAN BUS FLEETS: HybriDrive propulsion systems are providing clean transportation in the US, UK, and Canada

CLEANER PROPULSION: 10 million gallons of fuel saved, and 100,000 tons of CO_2 and 500 tons of NO_x prevented to date

GREATER EFFICIENCY: Fuel consumption is typically 20 percent to 30 percent lower compared to conventional diesel buses, varying according to duty cycle

WHAT'S NEXT?

BAE Systems' ongoing investment in its HybriDrive propulsion system includes: lightweight, cost-effective lithium-ion energy storage; advanced power controls; and, modular traction systems that promote acceptance into new markets and adoption by new equipment manufacturers. San Francisco estimates that its bus fleet will be emissions-free by 2020, and London has announced plans to convert its entire fleet to hybrid electric vehicles for the 2012 Summer Olympics. Fuel cell anti-idle and prime propulsion power systems are on the horizon, along with battery-electric zero-emission vehicles enabled by the HybriDrive propulsion system.

New Heights in Eco-Construction

Design a tower to incredible resource efficiency standards to reduce operating costs and increase the quality of life for tenants

INNOVATION
The tower incorporates eco-efficient designs, materials and sophisticated environmental technologies such as cogeneration plants

Generates cost savings and enables the building to command higher price premiums

SUSTAINABILITY
Numerous passive and active sustainability measures: from floor plans that maximize sunlight, to onsite renewable power, to a cooling system that makes ice at night during off-peak hours that is used to cool the building during the day

RESULT
The tower generates 70% of its own power, reduces energy consumption by 50%, water consumption by 50%, and has a zero carbon footprint

With a LEED-certified platinum rating, it sets a high standard for commercial building construction

DRIVERS

BIG BOLD STATEMENT: In addition to being the 2nd highest building in NYC, the architects and developers committed to building the most energy-efficient, water-saving, healthful office tower ever

BETTER ROI: Based on a 2006 survey, green buildings have higher rental income due to 3.5% higher occupancy rate and 3% higher rent and lower operating cost of 8%-9%, leading to better financial returns

MEANINGFUL CSR: In 1998, the firm made an unprecedented 10-year, $350 billion commitment to corporate social responsibility — the Bank of America tower would become the largest initiative of the entire campaign

BARRIERS

HIGH COSTS: New York-area carting companies that haul out waste from construction sites charged extra to sort and recycle construction debris into steel, concrete and other material groupings

UNPROVEN TECHNOLOGY: Bank of America wanted to install waterless urinals which had been rarely seen or requested in New York City at the time of construction — the city's building code did not even allow them

WORKER RESISTANCE: Using new technology could mean less work for laborers, making unions reluctant to approve their implementation — an example is the plumber's union's objection to the implementation of waterless urinals

ENABLERS

HIGH VALUE OF WASTE: Since 90% of the BofA tower construction wastes can be recycled, the carting companies have realized their value — they lowered their prices and became more cooperative as a result

REGULATORY PUSH: New building codes for New York city based on international building codes were implemented in mid 2007 — they now allow for waterless urinals as long as they are part of a larger water-saving design

IMPROVING TECHNOLOGY: The implementation of new technology such as a rainwater collection and distribution piping system will mean even more work than installing traditional systems, which will satisfy labor unions

IMPACT

BETTER WORKPLACE: Energy and water savings are estimated to reach a minimum of 50% and productivity gains will reach 10-15% due to cleaner air, more daylight and a more comfortable work environment

PRIME REAL ESTATE: Despite the high rent cost and the recession, the tower was 98% leased by 2007, attracting firms such as General Investment Management to its environmental and architectural innovations

THE GREEN APPLE: Green design has become the trend in New York — the BofA tower is joined by others such as the Hearst Tower, 7 WTC and the New York Times HQ as symbols for environment-focused architecture

WHAT'S NEXT?

After opening in 2009, the eco-friendly design, construction and operation of the Bank of America Tower will make it the first skyscraper to receive the highest sustainability certification — Platinum — by the US Green Building Council's LEED rating system.

Steel Waste into Revenue Streams

A ten year project to design and implement an efficient recycling and reuse program for slag—the by-product of steel production

INNOVATION
A process—BSSF—to quickly cool and recycle steel slag that minimizes waste that falls on the production floor and eliminates the need to bury the waste in the ground for up to one year for cooling

SUSTAINABILITY
BSSF eliminates the potential for buried slag to pollute soil and water

Higher recovery rates of iron ore from slag and removal of limestone from the process, which is traditionally used when slag is buried

RESULTS
In addition to reducing the potential environmental impact, the BSSF process saves 400,000 tons of iron ore and 533,000 tons of limestone per year for Baosteel

DRIVERS

TACKLE THE ELEPHANT: Baosteel, the 3rd largest steel producer globally, buried over 1.6 m tons of slag per year as part of a one-year cooling process that risked ground contamination

BIG BOLD STATEMENT: Recognizing the need to improve efficiency and reduce its overall environmental impact, the firm set a goal to become a "world-class clean steel enterprise"

COST DRIVEN: Recycling one ton of slag is equal to saving 250kg iron ore and 330kg limestone; moreover, one ton of molten slag contains heat energy equivalent to 60kg coal

GOVERNMENT PUSH: Baosteel signed contracts with state and regional governments that set ambitious energy-saving and total pollutant goals

BARRIERS

TECHNICAL BARRIERS: The process m known as "BSSF" raised new technical barriers, including the need to reduce explosion risk caused by sudden expansion of water during the quick cooling of scorching slag

COMPANY SILOS: The slag problem touched multiple parts of the steel production process and the firm — coordinating frequent industrial trials and maintaining production schedules slowed the project

REAL TESTING ENVIRONMENT: The industrialization and optimization of BSSF technology requires experience from real world application, but Baosteel did not have enough projects to conduct meaningful tests

ENABLERS

LONG TERM R&D INVESTMENT: Baosteel invested in the BSSF project for 13 years, developing new technologies and slag preprocessing techniques to overcome the explosion risk and other barriers encountered

SENIOR SPONSOR: A senior executive took control of the BSSF R&D project and secured direct responsibility for helping the project team coordinate efforts across the company

PARTNERSHIP: Baosteel established a technology trade platform to work with other steel companies to test the processes and share knowledge across companies

IMPACT

ENVIRONMENT: CO_2 and SO_2 emissions and dust caused by steel slag is totally eliminated, thus reducing the environmental impact of the steel plants

COMPANY: The BSSF process improves the metal recovery rate by 30% and the break even for the equipment investment is as short as half a year

GLOBAL RECOGNITION: In 2007 BSSF won the 2nd prize at the China National Invention Awards and the 1st prize at the International Innovation Expo held in Hamburg, Germany

INDUSTRY: BSSF is now widely used by other steel companies in China, such as Masteel and Nanchang Steel, and was exported to JSW Steel in India

WHAT'S NEXT?

Baosteel originally designed the BSSF slag process for the steel industry and is now exploring the potential application of the technology to other metallurgic industries.

Modular Batteries for Electric Cars

Overcoming the high cost and low range problems of electric vehicles with leased, swappable batteries and a network of charging stations

INNOVATION

100% electric vehicles (EV) with leasable battery packs that spread the cost of batteries on a per-mile or fixed monthly recharge plan

Uses swappable batteries and automated replacement stations that switch a battery in under two minutes

SUSTAINABILITY

100% EVs substantially reduce dependency on fossil fuels for motor vehicle use

Battery stations charge batteries overnight when electric grids have cheaper underutilized energy

RESULTS

Up to a 70% per-mile drop in transport costs compared to gas-powered vehicles and an estimated 21% reduction of CO_2 emissions

Raised over $500 million to build service stations in Israel and Denmark to serve cars made by Renault

DRIVERS

OFF-PEAK ENERGY UTILIZATION: Current underutilization of electric grids drove Better Place to find a way for EVs to maximize this resource — a majority of domestic vehicles could be replaced by EVs without increasing electricity supply

GOVERNMENT INCENTIVES: A range of grants, tax breaks, pending regulations and stimulus funds by governments around the world created a pile of money for hybrid- and 100% EV-related companies

DEMAND PULL: The success of the Toyota Prius and other hybrids demonstrated that customers are interested in more efficient alternatives to internal combustion engines

BARRIERS

CAPTURING UNUSED ENERGY: There is a current lack of technology and systems in place that allow for capturing unused electricity as well as ensuring the proper management and distribution of underutilized energy

CHICKEN OR THE EGG: While 100% EVs are more efficient than gas-electric hybrids, their short, 100-mile range requires a network of charging locations — but without a large group of customers, building the infrastructure would be too risky

UPFRONT COSTS: As with hybrid vehicles, the lithium ion battery packs used in 100% EVs add significant upfront costs to the vehicle, making the cars too expensive for most customers

ENABLERS

IMPROVING TECHNOLOGY: The firm developed a system of swappable batteries and a network of replacement stations that collect energy in racks of batteries at night and function like traditional gas stations for their vehicles

NOT WHAT, BUT WHERE: Better Place identified and sought partnerships with the governments of densely populated, self-contained regions including Israel, Hawaii and Denmark where the infrastructure investment would be minimal

NEW BUSINESS MODEL: Better Place adopted the 'cell-phone' business model to help reduce the high purchase price of EV cars — customers pay for energy on a per mile basis or fixed rate plan for unlimited miles or battery swaps

IMPACT

INDUSTRY: The combo of new business models and new technologies indicates there can be a range of product and service offerings for more eco-friendly vehicles as in the computer and mobile phone industries

SCALABLE SOLUTIONS: By demonstrating the success in its pilot regions, Better Place hopes to scale its solution to larger and less dense areas as it moves down the cost curve — Japan, California, and Australia have now signed up

INVESTORS: In early 2010, Better Place received a substantial market validation by raising over $350 million in funding, valuing the company at over $1.25 billion — this money will be used to build out its infrastructure

WHAT'S NEXT?

Although Better Place has signed on Renault to produce the initial EV, it is actively looking to engage other major auto manufacturers to produce compatible machines.

A Smarter, Solar Powered Trash Can

Reducing trash collection frequency with off-grid, solar-powered trash compactors that alert disposal companies when full

INNOVATION

Trash compactors powered by solar cells have 5x more capacity than non-compacting trash cans

Sensors measure remaining capacity and send text messages to let the system know when they are full

SUSTAINABILITY

Solar cells enable the compactor to operate with no carbon footprint

Unnecessary trips by garbage trucks to empty half-full cans are eliminated, creating a more efficient trash removal process

RESULTS

Municipalities that formerly emptied garbage cans daily now empty BigBelly trash cans once a week, leading to fewer trips by garbage trucks and decreasing fuel use and emissions by 80%

The city of Philadelphia had an immediate cash flow savings of $1 million in the first year and an estimated $10 million in 10 years

DRIVERS

LEADER'S VISION: Jim Poss developed the concept for BigBelly Solar by combining his experience in electric vehicle engineering and enthusiasm for finding greener solutions to traditional problems

TACKLE THE ELEPHANT: US garbage trucks consume over one billion gallons of diesel each year and averages two mpg, making them some of the most expensive, fuel-intensive and inefficient vehicles to operate on a per unit basis

URBANIZATION: Higher population densities lead to increases in trash which can overwhelm the ability of traditional trash collection systems to operate efficiently and to ensure trash is collected when required

BARRIERS

WORKER RESISTANCE: Workers in the waste management industry were initially concerned with a new trash compaction system that would require fewer trips for garbage trucks and less work for them

MISLEADING DATA: An environmental website incorrectly asserted that the firm's trash compactors would reduce oxygen for landfill-based micro-organisms, thereby increasing trash decomposing time in landfills

CONFUSED PUBLIC: When BigBelly was initially installed in selected cities, some people either had no idea what it was or mistook it for a package delivery company's drop box

ENABLERS

LOCAL SUPPORT: Densely populated neighborhoods concerned about growing litter problems have helped push for the installation of these trash compactors to reduce the time that trash cans remain full

EDUCATION: Initial claims of the website were refuted both by the website itself and BigBelly by citing EPA articles that the technology does not inhibit sorting, recycling or decomposing in landfills

RECOGNIZABLE DESIGN: The company created a new design for the trash can that would make it more attractive and included explicit, standardized signage to make the purpose of the compactor more obvious

IMPACT

CITY BUDGETS: Tim McCarthy of Boston Public Works said, "City time and money saved can now be allotted to other projects, such as filling potholes and fixing sidewalks"

INTERNAL: The company has been growing at 400% annually since its inception; it is poised for continued growth with its wireless system

CITY PRESENCE: Big Belly compactors are now present in 46 states including Boston, Seattle, Chicago, Philadelphia and New York and 30 countries, contributing to their waste- and energy-reduction strategies

WHAT'S NEXT?

After successfully demonstrating the consumer version of the product for parks and cities, BigBelly is working on a larger-scale version of its trash compactor for industrial use.

A Fuel Cell Breakthrough?

Together with a wide range of partners, Bloom Energy aims to revolutionize distributed energy generation with a new, cost-effective fuel cell technology

INNOVATION

A proprietary coating and production method creates a cost-effective fuel cell that converts air and nearly any fuel source into electricity

Bloom has built a powerful network of public and private sector investors, champions and lead customers like eBay and Google to support the scale-up of its business

SUSTAINABILITY

The electro-chemical power generation process is 67-100% cleaner (depending on the fuel) than a coal-fired power plant

Cleaner than traditional electricity generation and more reliable than solar and wind power which can be sporadic

RESULTS

Since commercial roll-out began in 2002, the systems produced more than 11 million kWh of electricity since July 2008 — the equivalent of powering 1,000 homes for a year

This translates into 14 million less pounds of CO_2 compared to using coal power

DRIVERS

TECHNOLOGY PUSH: KR Sridhar, the CEO and Founder of Bloom, invented a system for NASA to generate oxygen and hydrogen on Mars — the project was canceled but reversing the process would create energy as a fuel cell

LEADER'S VISION: KR Sridhar believed that finding new ways to more efficiently generate electricity is critical to enabling future generations to have a better life than the past

INITIAL INVESTMENT: Kleiner, Perkins, Caulfield & Byers, a venerated VC firm, provided Bloom with the required capital to get started in 2002 and has invested a total of $250 million in the company

BARRIERS

NEW INDUSTRY: Bloom Energy needs large investments over a long time horizon to scale an entire supply chain around its product. The economic crisis exacerbated the issue

SCEPTICS: In the past other fuel cell ventures could not achieve breakthrough commercial success and the past failures color future investment and development decisions

HIGH PRICE: A 100kWh system currently costs $700,000, putting it out of reach of most customers and limiting the potential for Bloom Energy to reach a profitable scale

ENABLERS

PUBLIC & PRIVATE SUPPORT: Despite the financial crisis Bloom successfully raised an additional $150 million; the US Department of Energy also stepped in and provided valuable loan guarantees that enabled Bloom to move forward

LEAD CUSTOMERS: Bloom Energy convinced 20 leading Fortune100 companies, like Google, eBay, Wal-Mart and others to trial the technology and provide high profile references

NEW TECHNOLOGIES: The use of cheap materials, a proprietary coating and a new production method allows Bloom Boxes to be more easily mass-produced driving down the price

IMPACT

ENVIRONMENT: By saving the energy lost during the typical combustion process and the distribution through the grid, the system is ~67-100% cleaner (depending on the fuel) than energy generated in coal-fired power plants

CUSTOMERS: Estimates suggest that customers can expect a 3-5 year payback on their capital investment from the energy cost savings, and achieve a 40-100% reduction in CO_2 emission compared with using the grid

INDUSTRY: With its new product and public and private support, Bloom Energy reignited the discussion about the potential for fuel cells as a step in the direction of more efficient energy production

WHAT'S NEXT?

Bloom Energy's ultimate goal is to put a Bloom Box in every household in 5-10 years by scaling up production and drastically lowering the price. Besides on-site energy generation, there is a large range of other possible future applications, including on-board systems for vehicles

BOMBARDIER

Quieter, More Fuel Efficient Jets
Establishing new benchmarks in aviation sustainability with the CSeries mid-sized aircraft

INNOVATION
A new series of airplanes leverages novel technologies from a supplier to reduce costs and push forward on new benchmarks in aviation sustainability

Higher costs were mitigated with a customer leasing option

SUSTAINABILITY
Pratt and Whitney's next-generation geared turbofan engine was instrumental in driving down fuel consumption by 20%

The advancement from this collaboration created over 3,000 new jobs in manufacturing plants

RESULTS
20% reduction in fuel consumption

Reduced noise

20% fewer carbon emissions

50% fewer nitrous oxide emissions during flight

© copyright 2010 IXL Center

DRIVERS

CUT MY COSTS: Because of rising fuel costs and operating expenditures faced by airline companies, Bombardier sought new ways to drive down operational costs

REGULATORY PUSH: With tightening airline regulations and a need for airlines to meet demands with less environmental impact, Bombardier saw an opportunity to design a new generation of green planes

UNMET NEED: While most airlines flew planes with a capacity either below 100 seats or above 150 seats, there were few flights seating between 100-149 passengers — Bombardier saw this as a new opportunity to pursue

BARRIERS

ORGANIZATIONAL STRUCTURE: Investing in new technologies was not a focal point of the company — in poor economic times, the tendency had been to look at: short-term savings; cutting down on workforce; or, shutting down plants

CROSS BORDER CONCERNS: Traditionally, the airline industry was known for its unbending engineering and technical standards, which made some of the new technology in the CSeries difficult to sell

LACK OF BUYERS: Bombardier's CSeries was seemingly high-priced for customers facing tight credit markets and tough economic times — there was a lack of potential buyers to secure firm orders

ENABLERS

HORIZONTAL INTEGRATION: In an effort to design new efficient technologies at minimal costs, Bombardier looked to its suppliers to aid in the development — Pratt and Whitney's next-generation "geared turbofan engine" showed promise

CORPORATE VISION: Because of the growing emphasis of sustainability, Bombardier knew that airlines would have to become more creative to reduce emissions in order to avoid costly regulatory charges and re-tooling in the future

LEASE ME INSTEAD: Bombardier introduced a new lease option for airlines unable to pay the full price of the CSeries planes — this gave airlines an opportunity to test the new airplane at a low investment cost

IMPACT

TECHNOLOGY: Successful new technologies in design and aerodynamics helped to drive down fuel costs by 20% and to create over 3,000 new jobs at a time when competitors were scaling back their operations

SUSTAINABLE CUSTOMERS: With a focus on building a fleet of sustainable jets, companies such as Lufthansa have affirmed their efforts in aviation sustainability by offering flights with reduced emissions, lower noise and less fuel burn

OFF THE SHELF: Decreased price barriers kick-started production of the CSeries, which encouraged Lufthansa to buy 30 planes and to lease another 30 — letters of intent from other airlines soon followed suit

WHAT'S NEXT?

Building on technologies capable of producing 20% less CO_2, 50% less NO_x, 20% less fuel burn and less noise, Bombardier will apply this blueprint of airline efficiency across all its other models in an effort to build a more sustainable aviation industry.

Start/Stop System for Hybrids

Enhances fuel efficiency and reduces noise pollution caused by the internal combustion engine of a hybrid while preserving driving comfort

INNOVATION
The start/stop system switches off the internal combustion engine when the vehicle is stationary — for example, in traffic jams or at red lights — and switches it back on when the driver releases the brake pedal

SUSTAINABILITY
Depending on the vehicle, start/stop systems help to save fuel, resulting in producing less CO_2 in stop-and-go traffic and urban sites while decreasing noise pollution

RESULTS
While idling, 96% of CO_2 emissions are cut and up to 8% of fuel consumption is saved by turning off the engine

One million vehicles have now been fitted with Bosch's start/stop technology since production began in 2007

DRIVERS

TACKLE THE ELEPHANT: According to a report by NRDC, motor vehicles are the second largest source of CO_2 pollution, creating about 1.5 billion tons of CO_2 and contributing to global warming and health problems

NOISE POLLUTION: Most outdoor noise worldwide is created by transportation systems, including motor vehicles — noise pollution can increase stress, cause sleep problems and produce other harmful health problems

REGULATORY PUSH: Worldwide emission standards set specific limits on the amount of pollutants that can be released by cars — regulations became stricter over time, forcing car makers to invest in alternative technologies

BARRIERS

DRIVING EXPERIENCE: Critical issues included product refinement and driver confidence — the start/stop system cannot afford to irritate the driver through slow response or by faltering

ELECTRIC POWER DEMAND: At first, this invention seemed like just one more of the growing number of technologies in modern passenger cars that place increasing demands on the automotive charging systems

ECONOMIC DOWNTURN: Because of the financial crisis, motor vehicle sales dropped an average of 35% and manufacturers have had to operate with less funds available for R&D

ENABLERS

INNOVATIVE ENGINEERING: Integrated starter-alternator systems aim to balance out irregularities in running engines, providing more comfort — thanks to clever electronics, starting is fast and reliable

EFFICIENT ALTERNATOR: The highly efficient alternator designed by Bosch needs less mechanical energy to create the required amount of electrical energy

LOW TECHNICAL EXPENSES: The start/stop technology combines existing technologies, therefore offers a good route for automakers to reduce emissions and meet CO_2 reduction targets at rather modest technical expense

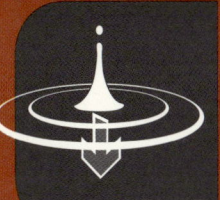

IMPACT

CUSTOMERS: According to research, vehicles are at a standstill for one-third of the time while in urban areas — with the rise in oil prices, high fuel efficiency leads to an excellent cost/benefit ratio

ENVIRONMENT: Start/stop systems adopted by many motor vehicles result in massive reductions in fuel costs, emissions and noise pollution

INTERNAL: Since production began, more than one million cars have been equipped with the technology, making Bosch the market leader in start/stop systems

WHAT'S NEXT?

According to forecasts, European CO_2 emissions regulations will quickly spur the growth of start/stop systems so that 50% of all newly registered vehicles will be equipped with them — most manufactured by Bosch.

'Oorja' Smokeless Biomass Stove

Target a unique emerging market need with an affordable, clean and safe cooking solution that reduces carbon emissions, with a proven sales model, in India

INNOVATION
BP Energy's smokeless biomass stove for rural India uses a rechargeable mini-fan to increase efficiency vs. existing wood stoves

Direct sales model is similar to approaches used in other industries (e.g., microlending with Grameen Bank)

SUSTAINABILITY
By using biomass pellets, the stove's emissions are greatly reduced, lowering global warming pressures and preserving human health

Provides a promising answer to the rising total emissions in India

RESULTS
Reduces carbon monoxide by 71% and lessens suspended particulate matter by 34% compared to traditional wood-burning stoves

Provides new streams of income for emerging women entrepreneurs in India

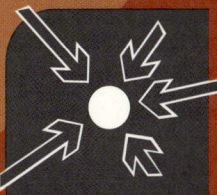

DRIVERS

TACKLE THE ELEPHANT: India is ranked fourth in the world in creating harmful emissions — traditional wood-burning stoves commonly used in rural areas are responsible for a significant portion of carbon emissions

HEALTH ISSUES: Indoor air pollution related to wood-burning stoves kills nearly 400,000 people in India each year, according to the World Heath Organization

DEMAND PULL: Using wood slows the cooking process because of additional tasks such as wood collecting. Existing alternatives like kerosene and liquefied petroleum gas are too expensive and very flammable

BARRIERS

CHANGE OF MINDSET: The company needed to create a different business model and cater to different customer needs — the Indian market challenged the existing cost structures and price performance of the company

POVERTY: Economies of scale due to large demand and mass production could lower the price of the stove, but people in rural India may still not be able to afford it because of extreme poverty

DISTRIBUTION: Targeted customers, the rural poor, could not be reached by the traditional distribution channels

ENABLERS

COMMITTED PARTNERS: BP Energy India, members of non-governmental organizations, scientists, local entrepreneurs, and end users worked together to design, manufacture, and market the stove

IMPROVING TECHNOLOGY: Because of efficient material use, the stove costs only about $17; making it affordable for customers of emerging markets — also, a mini-fan blows air to increase combustion efficiency

DIRECT SALES: Local women, who are trusted by their community, are recruited to sell the stoves — their feedback taught BP about the challenges of rural marketing in a extremely diverse nation

IMPACT

ENVIRONMENT: The stove reduces carbon monoxide by 71% and lessens suspended particulate matter by 34% compared to traditional wood-burning stoves

CUSTOMERS: Cooking takes less time because biomass pellets burn more efficiently than wood — annual biomass use would fall from 1.5 - 2 to 0.4 - 0.6 tons per family

SALES FORCE: The sales of new stoves and the supply of the healthier smokeless fuel pellets provide a sustainable income source for rural women

INTERNAL: There are hundreds of thousands of stoves in operation at the moment and BP believes it can sell 20 million by 2020

WHAT'S NEXT?

Based on the positive experience in India, BP will also test the stove in Vietnam and China.

All Natural Personal Care Products

Producing high quality personal care products using natural ingredients and minimal processing to decrease environmental impact

INNOVATION

Burt's Bees replaces synthetic chemicals and processes with natural ingredients and minimal processing but still achieves the very competitive quality in personal care products

SUSTAINABILITY

Impact to the environment is minimized because only ingredients from renewable resources found in nature are used in Burt's Bees products — also, they are packaged with post-recycled or biodegradable materials

RESULTS

Burt's Bees' 150 products on average are 99% natural

The company experienced more than 300% growth from 2002 to 2007, selling over 60 million units annually

DRIVERS

SERENDIPITY: Founders Roxanne Quimby and Burt Shavitz produced only candles until Roxanne found a 19th century book of home-made personal care recipes, thus adding natural personal care products to their portfolio

DEMAND PULL: Burt's Bees started expanding their product line of natural personal care products from soaps and perfumes to lip balm and other skin care products to keep up with the trend to use all natural ingredients

COMMITTED PARTNER: In 2007, Burt's Bees was acquired by Clorox, expanding the global reach of their products, increasing brand awareness and bringing more operational efficiency and technology to their operations

BARRIERS

WHAT IS NATURAL?: Lacking a shared definition of what exactly is "natural" limits the impact of Burt's Bees products because other products can also display "natural" labels while not maintaining similar high standards

PRODUCTION CAPACITY: An abandoned bowling alley in Maine where 40 employees manufactured their products was not enough to meet the increasing number of customer orders

HALO EFFECT: There were fears that the acquisition would affect Burt's Bees negatively as Clorox is controversial among environmentalists and animal rights activists

ENABLERS

STANDARDS ORGANIZATION: Burt's Bees spearheaded the effort to establish The Natural Standard for Personal Care Products together with their suppliers and competitors to define what is natural and which products can be labeled as such

EXPANSION: In 1994, Burt's Bees increased their production capacity by moving to an 18,000 foot former garment factory in Creedmoor, NC and automating their operations

TRANSPARENCY: Burt's Bees released its first-ever Corporate Social Responsibility report, assuring customers that they are sticking to their principles of using only natural ingredients and processes

IMPACT

SEAL AND SYMBOLS: All Burt's Bees products now carry a Natural Products Association seal to assure customers that the Natural Standard is met along with a "Natural Bar" to indicate the % of natural ingredients in its products

INTERNAL: The company was able to grow sales from $20,000 in 1984 to $8 million in 1998 with more than 4,000 unique products (SKUs) sold in over 4,000 retail outlets

GLOBAL PRESENCE: Burt's Bees products are now available globally through Clorox with over $300 million in sales in 2007, showing that customers still trust and use Burt's Bees products

WHAT'S NEXT?

Burt's Bees aims to grow 300% every 3 years while reducing environmental impact in all company operations by striving to be carbon free, operate on 100% renewable energy and produce products that are 100% natural.

COMPANIES INNOVATING TO CREATE A MORE SUSTAINABLE WORLD

Bioremediating Parts Washing System

Cost-effective parts washing system, ChemFree's SmartWasher replaces hazardous solvents with a natural, water-based biological solution

INNOVATION

A combination of non-hazardous cleaning fluids and specially-developed microbes that "eat" oil and grease

The cleaner cleans the parts and the microbes clean the cleaner, resulting in a long-term supply of safe, effective, pollutant-free cleaning fluid

SUSTAINABILITY

SmartWasher replaces traditional solvents, eliminating the creation of liquid hazardous wastes and the use and transport of caustic, flammable and potentially toxic materials

A properly maintained system may never require fluid to be changed

RESULTS

ChemFree's solution is a parts washer that works as well or better than traditional parts cleaning systems, costing 20%—50% less to operate (after capital acquisition costs) while avoiding cradle-to-grave liability for conventional solvents mandated by EPA

DRIVERS

TACKLE THE ELEPHANT: A traditional solvent-based parts washer is estimated to produce air pollution that is equivalent to ten cars running 24 hours-a-day — there are over 1.5 million such washers in use in the US

SEED CAPITAL: In 1993, co-inventors of the SmartWasher convinced an incubator firm to underwrite research based on the unique use of microbes to replace solvents

REGULATIONS: The prospect of EPA regulations led large corporations and government agencies to look for better solutions to traditionally toxic processes like parts washing

CHANGE THE STATUS QUO: Most parts washer customers leased systems from service providers to handle waste disposal — eliminating solvents could enable a new direct sales model

BARRIERS

RESISTANCE TO CHANGE: Customers were reluctant to make the shift from leasing to buying a new kind of parts washer from an untested supplier

PERFORMANCE: The first generation system did not perform as well as traditional solvent-based systems that customers trusted

LACK OF STANDARDS: Without existing standards for water-based cleaning systems, there was no way to get the system approved by the largest potential customers like the military

VALUE CHAIN: Chemfree focused on going directly to customers but got relatively little traction — traditional service providers "owned" the relationship

ENABLERS

LEAD CUSTOMERS: Chemfree persuaded a national auto aftermarket sales group to represent the SmartWasher, enabling the system to reach a wide range of potential customers

CONTINUED R&D: Increasing effectiveness of the microbial technology enabled the solution to reach 99% effectiveness of traditional mineral spirits solvents

SPREAD THE WORD: Chemfree added greater focus to the lease/service distribution channel, ensuring that all of the parties in the value chain understood the power of the SmartWasher system

COMMITTED PARTNER: By teaming with a service company to deliver its sustainable parts washing system with a service component, the system reached and succeeded with even more customers

IMPACT

GREENER CUSTOMERS: Convinced that sustainable parts washers can do a great job, many customers now buy greener products for other maintenance jobs

CHANGING THE MARKET: Success and acceptance of the SmartWasher products have forced the competition to introduce less hazardous products

INTERNAL: ChemFree now sells its products in more than 40 countries and holds 27 patents, 11 in the United States and 16 in other countries

WIN-WIN: The partnership with a service company enabled the company to double its domestic and international market share in less than two years

WHAT'S NEXT?

ChemFree is expanding into new markets and new product areas with a global roll out of its service partnership concept and the development of more effective sustainable cleaning solutions that meet international aircraft standards as well as general cleaning products and low temperature microbial cleaners.

Device-Level Energy Management

Any electronic device connected to a corporate network can be individually optimized to consume less energy

INNOVATION
A system that can identify power consumption patterns at the device level and optimize power usage on an enterprise scale (instead of managing devices individually)

SUSTAINABILITY
The system helps firms create energy management programs and schedules that reduce electricity use and increase cost savings of any networked device

RESULTS
For small to mid-sized offices, Cisco EnergyWise can yield a 50% potential annual energy and cost savings as well as a reduced carbon footprint

DRIVERS

COMPETITION:
A powerful 2008 campaign by Nortel claimed companies were paying a "Cisco Energy Tax" based on the poor energy efficiency of its devices — the company wanted to respond effectively

TACKLE THE ELEPHANT:
The company estimated that IT and building infrastructure (like HVAC systems) use 96% of a commercial building's electricity — relatively small improvements in IT power use could yield large absolute benefits

GOVERNMENT PUSH:
A 2009 survey found that 69% of data center executives said they were "extremely or very concerned" about government regulation related to energy use — preparing for the inevitable became a top priority

BARRIERS

SECURITY BREACH:
IT managers were wary of automating building systems and unifying them under one network management program due to the risk of attack and disruption of centralized systems

PROPRIETARY SYSTEM:
The original system did not work with non-Cisco devices or with building infrastructure, discouraging potential customers from making large investments in a new product that could lock them in

BETTER ALTERNATIVES?:
Implementing an automated energy management system is expensive and may not yield as much improvement as investing in more energy efficient devices and consolidating infrastructure

ENABLERS

PILOT PROJECTS:
Those with Cisco software and devices can upgrade their system for free to add and test software, thus streamlining processes before conducting a full roll-out

COMMITTED PARTNER:
Cisco acquired a technology firm with software that managed multi-party facility management systems — the technology was adapted to make EnergyWise compatible with many other devices in the market

HOLISTIC APPROACH:
The firm promotes EnergyWise as one of several related tools it can deploy with customers, including energy-efficient data centers and energy-saving work practices such as virtualization and Telepresence

IMPACT

STANDARDS CREATION:
Cisco is using its experience with power management and other efficiency measures to align public and private stakeholders through the creation of common measures of energy efficiency for IT products

CUSTOMERS:
By providing a clearer picture of power-consumption habits across an organization, EnergyWise is changing the way companies organize, deploy and manage IT infrastructure

RELATED INDUSTRIES:
Cisco's entry into IT energy management created new opportunities in adjacent markets like smart grids where the company is actively developing partnerships push new industry standards

WHAT'S NEXT?

After incorporating support for many types and brands of IT equipment, the company is now developing the capability to manage building infrastructure systems like HVAC and lighting which account for the largest share of energy consumption in buildings.

COMPANIES INNOVATING TO CREATE A MORE SUSTAINABLE WORLD

Rapid Transit System in Curitiba, Brazil

An eco-friendly, reliable, efficiently constructed, cost effective bus transport system

INNOVATION

A flexible network of buses and stations that meets the needs of a rapidly growing urban environment without busting city budgets for capital investments in rail

Has the capacity to serve an unlimited range of locations throughout Curitiba, achieving the speed and efficiency of a subway system

SUSTAINABILITY

A highly reliable mass transport system that dramatically reduces automobile usage, fuel consumption and emission levels in the city

A versatile, cost- and time-effective model that can be implemented by making improvements to existing transport infrastructure and vehicles

RESULTS

A low cost transit system used by over 75% of travelers in Curitiba, a city of three million plus

Eliminates about 27 million automobile trips annually, saving 10 million gallons of fuel and lowering the city's CO_2 emissions by 25%

A model for developing cities worldwide

DRIVERS

POPULATION GROWTH: Curitiba's rapid population growth taxed the capacity of an antiquated electric trolley system, creating a dire need to improve the public transportation system

GOVERNMENT PUSH: The government wanted to stimulate economic growth for the urban population and to facilitate greater mobility by improving the transportation infrastructure

SERVICE CAPACITY: The outdated fare payment system and narrow bus doors created transportation bottlenecks, resulting in slow and inefficient service

BARRIERS

LEGACY CONSTRAINTS: The legacy electric trolley service followed fixed routes — expansion of service capacity to new routes was constrained by the narrow city streets and a tight municipal budget

ECONOMIC SETBACKS: Economic setbacks, including periods of hyperinflation, discouraged development of the roads necessary for an efficient bus transit system

TECHNOLOGY: The municipality lacked the technology to develop a system that could reduce congestion at bus terminals

ENABLERS

ADMINISTRATION: Mayor Moreira Garcez's commission for the streets permitted a local power company to explore the possibility of a bus network for the city

CUT MY COSTS: The Institute for Research and Urban Planning in Curitiba (IPPUC) constructed roads for buses at 1/10th the cost of laying a subway system, enabling systematic urban and economic development

DESIGN CHANGES: Cylindrical tube-shaped station enables passengers to make fare pre-payment; bus design permits commuters to board and exit buses simultaneously

IMPACT

BUS-ENABLED COMMERCE: The bus transport network better connects far-flung urban areas, increasing the trade and commerce within the city

BUILD ON SUCCESS: Mayor Ivo Aruza Prereir commissioned the IPPUC to plan a integrated transport system that will support further urban development

SPEEDY SERVICE: The city municipality reduced the passenger waiting time at the terminals to no more than 15 to 19 seconds per boarding—1/8th less than the original time

WHAT'S NEXT?

The city municipality continues to improve the efficiency of the transport system through installation of sensors in its buses and along public transportation routes. Also, the city municipality plans to utilize 100% alternate energy sources to lower emission levels.

COMPANIES INNOVATING TO CREATE A MORE SUSTAINABLE WORLD

Energy from Animal Waste

Reduce air, water and soil pollution from cow manure by converting it into biogas that can be an energy source for the community

INNOVATION

Disposing of cow manure without polluting the environment

Microbial cow manure digesters generate methane which is captured and used as a steady source of energy

SUSTAINABILITY

The process significantly reduces pollution related to cow manure disposal, gets rid of manure odor and produces natural gas which produces fewer CO_2 emissions than coal or oil when used as an energy source

RESULTS

Each manure digester facility produces fertilizer from by-products, reduces manure odor by 95% and can generate 775 kilowatts of energy from 800 cows — enough to power 600 homes

DRIVERS

LEADER'S VISION: In 1998, Dairyland launched its "Evergreen" renewable energy program to enable cooperative members to distribute renewable energy to consumers

LOW PRICE OF MILK: Steadily increasing production of milk has depressed the price forcing dairy farms to be find new ways of making money and staying competitive

REGULATORY PUSH: The rapid growth in the size of dairy farms has resulted in new laws governing the handling and disposal of cow manure and this, in turn, forces farmers to look for new ways to manage and dispose waste

BARRIERS

UPFRONT COSTS: Most farmers were reluctant to purchase a cow manure digester facility that costs $2 million and spend additional time and money to operate the facility

SCALE REQUIREMENTS: To make the cow manure digester economically feasible, a dairy farm has to have at least 800 cows and most farms have fewer than that number

EXISTING SYSTEM: To break even, electricity generated from cow manure should be sold at six cents per kilowatt hour, but most utilities want to pay only two cents per kilowatt hour

ENABLERS

COMMITTED PARTNERS: Dairyland collaborates with farmers by purchasing the biogas extracted and then handles distribution of the electricity, which eases the financial and time burden on the farmer

IMPROVING TECHNOLOGY: There are studies and experiments being conducted to create and determine the economic viability of cow manure digesters designed for smaller dairy farms with 200-300 cows

GOVERNMENT INCENTIVES: State grants and loan programs can reduce the cost of making electricity while state renewable portfolio standards require utilities to generate a certain amount of energy from renewable sources

IMPACT

ENVIRONMENT: The process helps the farmer solve environmental compliance issues in manure disposal and makes a major contribution to reducing odors from animal waste

INTERNAL: By using the solid by-product of the digesters as bedding for cows, a dairy farm can save up to $72k annually and get $16k in added revenue from carbon credits for reducing methane emissions

INDUSTRY: Some energy providers and technology firms in agricultural areas are discontinuing or phasing out older businesses to focus on converting animal waste to methane to create electricity

WHAT'S NEXT?

Because of renewable portfolio standards, the use of cow manure to generate electricity is being adopted by other states including Vermont, California and Colorado. Microgy, the company that builds the digesters, plans to take the technology to pig and poultry farms.

Cooking Oil Fuels Public Transport

Using recycled cooking oil as fuel makes public buses cheaper to operate and more environmentally friendly

INNOVATION

Fuel from recycled cooking oil specifically adapted to the most widely-used mode of public transport in the Philippines: the Jeepney

A partnership to support the eco-friendly business model that maintains profits for operators and drivers

SUSTAINABILITY

Cooking oil is a widely-available fuel alternative in the Philippines that does not fluctuate in price as dramatically as gasoline

Replacing gasoline reduces emissions and provides a smoother, more powerful ride

RESULTS

Mileage is improved by 20% and cost is reduced by an average of 28.5%, thereby increasing profits for operators and drivers

Cushions the impact of increasing fuel prices on local public transportation

DRIVERS

CIVIL SOCIETY PUSH: NGOs recognized how rising fuel prices made life more difficult for low-income drivers and the Filipino riding public — alternative fuel sources would reduce the burden on both groups

WASTED RESOURCE: Used cooking oil was dumped down the drain or reused by food vendors as additives in animal feeds, which was known to pose certain health risks to the consumers of those meat products

TACKLE THE ELEPHANT: As the most popular mode of transport, smoke-belching Jeepneys were a major source of local pollution and public dissatisfaction

TECHNOLOGY: A range of attempts to develop used oil as an energy source — from straight blending to biodiesel conversion — were being introduced and touted as solutions

BARRIERS

FEAR OF THE UNKNOWN: Bus drivers feared losing their only source of income if these new fuel mixtures damaged their engines

ORGANIZED SOURCING: This cooking oil was easily sourced from major local fast food chains, but efficient collection in smaller restaurants and residential areas remained a challenge

AMBIGUOUS DATA: Though scientific literature on recycling cooking oil existed, data specific to Jeepneys did not exist, which inhibited immediate deployment until the right mix and price for mass consumption was determined

LACK OF STANDARDS: Product standards for biodiesel were defined, but would be too stringent for cooking oil-based fuels, which further limited their use

ENABLERS

PARTICIPANT GUARANTEE: For Jeepney operators who tested the technology, Don Bosco Technical College and iBOP Asia provided compensation for downtime, lost revenue and damage caused by the technology

SYNERGIES: Fast food chains agreed to sell recycled oil at 30% below the market rate while involvement of Jeepney associations, local government units, and the private sector made organized sourcing of cooking oil possible

COLLABORATIVE TESTING: A collaborative scientific process with the Jeepney sector to improve performance, durability and economic viability built trust to produce the best solution for the socio-economic landscape in the Philippines

BANNING RE-USE: Recognizing the ill effects of reusing cooking oil in restaurants and in animal feeds, an ordinance was passed prohibiting those practices, thus making the oil more widely available

IMPACT

OIL PRICE HIKE CUSHION: The use of cooking-oil-based fuel cushions the negative impact of oil price hikes on the income of the Jeepney drivers and operators

SUPPLEMENTAL INCOME: Jeepney associations obtain additional income from the collection, processing, sales and use of fuel made from used cooking oil

HEALTH: Avoided carcinogenic effects and other health risks of incorporating used cooking oil in food and in animal feeds

ENVIRONMENT: Displacement of fossil fuels by bio-based oils reduces global warming and acidification impacts of Jeepneys

WHAT'S NEXT?

The Don Bosco and iBOP Asia Waste cooking oil project will be expanded to cover more Jeepneys, local government units (LGUs) and transportation associations for a full nationwide implementation. A wider, more institutionalized system for the collection, processing and distribution of waste cooking oil and the creation of regulatory standards is expected.

Merry-Go-Round Powered Schools

Empower Playgrounds' electricity-generating playgrounds and LED lanterns transform playtime into electric power for learning

INNOVATION
Empower Playgrounds' equipment uses kinetic energy generated by kids' playtime activities to make power available at night to light classrooms in rural, off-the-grid villages in Africa

SUSTAINABILITY
The playgrounds provide a reliable and renewable clean source of electricity and an alternative to the light of kerosene lamps for education and development in rural regions

RESULTS
As of 2010, ten merry-go-rounds have been installed in Ghanaian schools, each supporting 18-30 lights, impacting the education of some 900 children and the number is growing

DRIVERS

CUSTOMER PULL: Founder Ben Markham needed to find a means to generate power and provide light for studying in African villages during his church mission in Ghana

ENHANCE EDUCATION: The founder also wanted to make learning more engaging and recreational for young students and to provide access to hands-on science labs

ECONOMIC DEVELOPMENT: Markham aimed to provide manufacturing know-how and local job opportunities for the citizens of Ghana by basing the manufacturing and administration of the organization within the country

BARRIERS

NEED FOR A TEAM: Markham invented the idea of using kid energy to generate electricity, but he possessed neither the team nor the detailed knowledge to execute his vision

MATERIAL SUPPLY: To enable mass production, the playground equipment had to be built using parts that were affordable and readily available in Ghana

UPFRONT COSTS: At a cost over $3500 each, the merry-go-round is difficult to fund for most schools and communities in Africa

ENABLERS

COMMITTED PARTNERS: Ben Markham partnered with Brigham-Young University (his alma mater) to create student teams that would develop the equipment and the curriculum for science education of the villagers

REUSE WHAT YOU CAN: To overcome the lack of materials, engineers developed a design that repurposed used auto parts and steel from the markets of Ghana

DONOR FUNDING: Empower Playgrounds has been registered in the US as a public charity so it can accept donations from around to world to fund manufacturing

IMPACT

EXTERNAL: Empower Playgrounds made the first step to provide electricity for segments of the African population that would otherwise not have access to electric power

SOCIAL ASPECTS: In cooperation with BYU and Ghana's ministry of education, the organization is developing a science curriculum to improve education delivery and to train Ghanaian students on how to problem-solve

INTERNAL: Designing and manufacturing the equipment provide hands-on engineering experience, attracting interns and Brigham Young University students to the organization

WHAT'S NEXT?

Empower Playgrounds is planning to install 25 more merry-go-round systems in 2010. In addition, a zip-line and a swing system that generate electricity are both under development to add more power-generating capabilities to playground equipment in schools.

Sunflowers for Solar Farms

A solar array that is easy to assemble and maintain, making solar farms more cost effective in most parts of the world

INNOVATION
The Sunflower highly concentrated photovoltaic (HCPV) system is pre-assembled and requires minimal maintenance to lower costs and deliver better efficiency (using triple junction cells) than traditional CPV systems

SUSTAINABILITY
Highly concentrated PV systems can already yield 1MW for every 5 acres of solar farm area, making solar farms an important component of a clean and sustainable energy source for the future

RESULTS
The Sunflower system has an industry-leading 29% conversion efficiency by focusing the suns rays with a concentration ratio of 1200:1 compared to 500:1 by traditional CPVs; its triple junction cells are 2.4 times less costly

DRIVERS

ELECTRIC UTILITIES: Increasing demand for modular approaches to solar farms that are grid-tied and efficient over the long term

INCENTIVES AND STANDARDS: Government incentives and the rapid adoption of renewable energy standards make solar farms more viable

IDEALAB AND FOUNDERS: The founders of Idealab, begun in 2001, are mission-driven to deliver cost-effective, grid-competitive solar electric power

BARRIERS

TECHNOLOGY EFFICIENCY: CPV and other systems efficiencies have hovered in the 15-20% range with associated high costs per watt delivered

UPFRONT COSTS: Highly customized solutions bring high costs in the absence of buy backs and/or standardized modules

UNPROVEN TECH AND SKEPTICISM: There is skepticism about the economics of solar power absent financial incentives as well as concern about new replacement technologies

ENABLERS

HCPV TECHNOLOGY: Increasing the concentration of solar rays from 500 : 1 up to 1,200 : 1 provides a major cost reduction when combined with high efficiency triple junction cells (38% more efficient than silicon cells)

SYSTEMS INTEGRATION: The Idealab approach to systems integration across a large range of disciplines includes advanced optics, cell thermal management, tracking systems design and robotic assembly

MODULAR MANUFACTURING: Low profile 10-module building blocks called "frame sets" are designed to minimize shipping and installation costs while maximizing flexibility for rooftop or graded land installations

IMPACT

SOLAR FARM INDUSTRY: Energy Innovations has been able to increase the concentration of its CPV system to 1,200:1, thereby requiring less than half the number of high cost cells used by competing systems

ENERGY COST AND BALANCE: The improvements in the cost of HCPV will significantly increase the ability of solar energy farms to become a major part of the overall energy equation in many parts of the world

LOW COST + HIGH EFFICIENCY: October 2009 announcement of world-leading 29% conversion efficiency is double the average of flat plate systems — combined with the focus on low costs, solar farms will become truly cost competitive

WHAT'S NEXT?

Continued improvements in triple junction cell efficiency combined with cost reduction programs in place are projected to continue to advantage this system relative to traditional thin film solar and crystalline silicon PV over the long term.

Paper-Thin Power Storage

Small, flexible batteries manufactured using non-toxic materials and low-cost printing technology suited for low-power applications

INNOVATION
Paper-thin, flexible battery cells that can be cheaply mass-produced enable the provision of low-power to a range of small one-time use applications like RFID tags, micro-sensors, cosmetic patches and beyond

SUSTAINABILITY
Unlike lithium, mercury and other battery chemistries, Enfucell's printed batteries contain no toxic substances, making them safely disposable in landfills and recyclable

RESULTS
Enfucell is actively marketing the printed battery globally with offices in Finland, France and the US and has partnered with a Finnish industry leader in RFIDs to create new products

DRIVERS

A BIG, AUDACIOUS GOAL:
Dr. Zhang, the founder of Enfucell, originally set out to research biofuels as a more environmentally friendly power source for batteries to replace traditional materials like lead, mercury, and cadmium

DEMAND PULL:
Bulky batteries limit the potential for RFIDs that interact with external "smart" systems; thus, there is a need for new technologies that can overcome this barrier

INNOVATIVE REGION:
Otaniemi is Finland's Silicon Valley where major tech universities, R&D centers and corporations (including Nokia) are co-located — Dr. Zhang studied biotech, researched biofuels and started Enfucell here

BARRIERS

HIGH COST:
After ten years of research, Dr. Zhang realized that even though batteries powered by biofuels can replace traditional batteries, the batteries would be far too expensive for commercial use

CHICKEN OR THE EGG:
Printed batteries do not yet have a volume application, making them less competitive without economies of scale, but companies are not willing to use this type of battery unless it is more cost-effective

LACK OF EXPERIENCE:
The founders of Enfucell were primarily scientists and researchers who wanted to commercialize the paper batteries concept but did not know how to get funding or set up a business

ENABLERS

FOCUS SHIFT:
Dr. Zhang then turned to low-powered fuel cells and in 2003 he created the first generation of paper batteries by combining a thin galvanic cell with paper printing and lamination technology

COMMITTED PARTNERS:
To develop new RFID applications, Enfucell has partnered and even moved into the same building as Auraprint Oy, a leading Finnish RFID and plastics label printer

FINANCIAL ADVISORS:
As Enfucell was spun out of the University of Helinski, the founders sought external help to secure seed funding — more funding from a government R&D organization enabled Enfucell to expand further

IMPACT

GLOBAL RECOGNITION:
The company has received several tech awards such as Technology Pioneers of 2007 at The World Economic Forum, helping the company gain visibility and create interest in its products

COMPANY:
In addition to smart RFIDs, Enfucell is finding new markets for printed batteries where it can get involved further down in the value chain with finished products such as cosmetic patches and greeting cards

INDUSTRY:
Firms like Enfucell are expected to expand downstream and develop unique applications for their printed batteries which will increase sales to an estimated $560 million in 2014

WHAT'S NEXT?

Enfucell continues to expand in focused markets — opening up a new office in Paris to serve the French hi-tech and cosmetic businesses, participating in the RFID Journal LIVE! 2009 event in Orlando, Florida and receiving new funding from private investors to continue product development.

Solid Waste to Energy

Radioactive and solid waste from medical and municipal sources is converted into clean energy and matter useful in building materials

INNOVATION
A self-sustaining plant, featuring a unique disposal technology that avoids burning, converts solid waste into two useful by-products: clean energy and building materials

SUSTAINABILITY
The plant leaves no surface water, groundwater, or soil pollution in its wake

The remaining waste material is inert and can be fully utilized for construction materials

RESULTS
EER's facilities have a capacity to convert 500 to 1,000 kilograms of waste per hour, almost ten times more than the existing industry solutions

About 70% of the energy powers the reactor and the remaining 30% is sold

DRIVERS

TACKLE THE ELEPHANT: About 600 million tons of municipal and industrial solid waste is generated annually by OECD countries — finding safe and effective disposal methods was a challenge

POOR ALTERNATIVES: Existing waste disposal solutions were half measures — landfills or incineration of waste still cause land, water or air pollution

EXISTING TECH: A process for treating low level radioactive waste was developed in Russia 20 years ago and EER believed it could be used with other waste streams

REGULATORY PUSH: Following fee increases associated with dumping hazardous waste in landfills, treatment options that had been off the table became viable

BARRIERS

HIGH COSTS: Building and operating waste management plants can be expensive with start-up costs, administrative fees as well as liability- and insurance-related expenditures

NEW REQUIREMENTS: While the new disposal technology looked promising, it could not be easily or inexpensively retrofitted into existing treatment plants

MARKET UNCERTAINTY: Waste management firms were skeptical that the new process would deliver significant benefits over the status quo

ENERGY REQS: The process required very high temperatures of up to 7,000°C, which would consume substantial amounts of energy

ENABLERS

FUNDING: EER attracted major Israeli, Japanese and Korean investment companies, providing substantial funding for the technology commercialization

PILOT PROJECT: EER built a test facility in Israel, enabling the firm to observe its operational, economic and environmental features

COMMITTED PARTNERS: EER partnered with a few leading waste disposal firms in the US, UK and other countries based on the results of the pilot plant

SYSTEM THINKING: EER devised a system that could capture and purify oxygen to provide clean fuel for a generator to maintain the required temperatures

IMPACT

MORE EFFECTIVE: The facilities are able to process between 500 kg and 1000 kg of waste per hour compared to other solutions that can only process up to 50 kg per hour

LOWER COSTS: The EER process costs $3,000 per ton, which is ten times less than the costs for conventional waste treatment

EXPANSION: EER has established subsidiaries in two target markets, Japan and Korea, marketing its waste treatment technology

SELF-SUSTAINING: The plant uses 70% of the generated electricity to drive its own operations, while 30% can be sold to nearby customers

WHAT'S NEXT?

After its initial success, EER is expanding globally and plans to build facilities in Europe, North America and Asia and is processing a greater variety of waste such as automotive residues, medical waste and other hazardous materials.

COMPANIES INNOVATING TO CREATE A MORE SUSTAINABLE WORLD

E-street

Intelligent Street Lighting

A cross-border partnership, in the EU, to create a market for "intelligent street lighting" to dramatically reduce energy consumption

INNOVATION
Organizations able to design, develop, finance, install and maintain lighting systems partnered to disseminate an "intelligent street lighting solution" that can be rapidly scaled up across Europe

SUSTAINABILITY
The new system—with dimmable lights as well as advanced communication administration and lighting monitors—reduces the level of light when needs are low, saves energy and cuts pollution

RESULTS
Over 20,000 street lights were installed over a 30 month pilot period—the project has identified an annual saving potential of 38 terawatt hours by retrofit of old installations, which is 64% of the present annual European consumption for street lights

DRIVERS

GOVERNMENT INCENTIVES: The Intelligent Energy — Europe (IEE) program was launched and financed by the European Union to save energy and to encourage the use of renewable energy sources

MARKET CREATION POTENTIAL: The identified business opportunities led to incenting many parties across the value chain who have expertise in street lighting to create a larger, more attractive market for "intelligent street lighting"

TACKLE THE ELEPHANT: The outdoor lighting systems for many European cities account for nearly 38 percent of their total energy use — rising energy prices created a need to develop more effective systems

BARRIERS

UNCERTAIN RISKS: One of the main barriers for retrofitting old street lighting systems is the lack of financial resources — including a lack of financial models among stakeholders to understand the true costs and benefits

SYSTEM MANAGEMENT: Introducing dynamic lighting also leads to more complex management system needs — especially for sophisticated, reliable, and well tested communication and data processing abilities

PUBLIC BUREAUCRACIES: The initial investment costs of major retrofit projects are high because of technology requirements and are generally not funded because street lighting is seen mainly as a public safety issue

ENABLERS

"TURN-KEY SOLUTION": As part of the program two companies developed a "turn-key solution" for investors which calculates investment, cost savings and cash flows

PILOT PROJECT: The first full-scale administrative tool piloted in Oslo provided a good template for E-Street because it leveraged existing infrastructure and deployed components widely to minimize risk

SCALE EFFECTS: After the pilot, increasing the number of units installed can significantly lower per-unit cost and deliver the economies of scale needed to drive financial savings and make the project affordable

IMPACT

ENVIRONMENT: The pilot in Oslo led to an annual reduction of 70% in energy consumption and 1,440 tons in CO_2 emissions compared to the burning of oil to provide electricity for 10,000 public street lights

CITIES AND REGIONS: The E-street project has identified an annual savings potential of 38 TWh by introducing/retrofitting old installations with adaptive lighting, cutting present annual European energy use up to 64%

SAFETY AND EFFICIENCY: The solution focuses on low energy consumption combined with a high functional standard — by reducing lamp downtime it has also significantly improved driver and pedestrian safety

WHAT'S NEXT?

The pilot project in the City of Oslo has become the basis for the E-Street initiative to reduce energy usage in outdoor lighting systems in the European Union. E-Street will play a pivotal role in determining EU standards and legislation for intelligent outdoor lighting systems.

Turning Landfill Gas into Electricity

The first landfill Clean Development Mechanism (CDM) project in Africa brings advanced solutions to developing world problems

INNOVATION
eThekwini Municipality (City of Durban) in partnership with the World Bank's Prototype Carbon Fund is running the first CDM certified land-fill to electricity project in Africa—this was made viable by selling carbon credits to developed countries

SUSTAINABILITY
The project converts landfill gas that is about 40-60% methane (CH_4) into electricity, reducing the reliance on coal-fired plants

CH_4 is 20-25 times more harmful than CO_2 as a green-house gas

RESULTS
In total, the project is expected to reduce equivalent emissions in CO_2 by 3.8 million tons

~450,000 tons out of the 3.8 million would have been emitted by alternative power generation over the project lifespan of the sites

DRIVERS

TACKLE THE ELEPHANT: CH_4 is 21 times more harmful than CO_2 to the environment and landfills and represents 5-15% of total CH_4 emissions; therefore, the problem of landfill gas emissions has to be addressed to reduce global warming

INTERNATIONAL PUSH: During the World Summit hosted by South Africa in 2002, Prototype Carbon Fund (PCF) — managed by the World Bank — suggested the development of a landfill gas utilization project to eThekwini

DEMAND FOR CARBON CREDIT: The emission limits set by the Kyoto Protocol — which entered into force in 2006 — raised the demand for carbon credits which were issued by the CDM as a certified emission saving project

BARRIERS

LACK OF EXPERIENCE: Durban Solid Waste (DSW), the municipal agency responsible for management and operation of the landfill sites, did not have the necessary experience in landfill gas utilization

NON-GREEN IS CHEAPER: From the munipality's point of view, a landfill-gas-to-electricity project is not attractive because purchasing electricity from the local provider is estimated to be about 66% cheaper on the long run in South Africa

ADMINISTRATION: Because of the lack of experience in CDM projects, the administration required to become a CDM-certified project and to sell carbon credits was underestimated both in terms of human resources and cost

ENABLERS

PARTNERSHIP: DSW started an advanced research collaboration with the University of KwaZulu-Natal to study the management of landfill gas emissions, which became internationally recognized

CARBON TRADING: The CDM, under the Kyoto Protocol, allowed project owners to generate an additional revenue stream through the sale of carbon credits to PCF, thus making the project financially viable

TEAMWORK: The dedication and passion of Lindsay Strachan (the DSW project manager), the full backing from the Mayor and the City Council, and the help of the Electricity Department resulted in a success story

IMPACT

ENVIRONMENT: According to an analysis, the project is able to realize a reduction of 7.7 million tons of CO_2 equivalent emissions by 2025, even though the PCF agreement is for the purchase of 3.8 million tons of reduction

MUNICIPALITY: The project will realize a net profit of $7.25 million over the expected agreement period of 12 years from the sale of carbon credits and the sale of electricity

RESIDENTS: The project improves the air quality and contributes to the protection of groundwater — these are particularly important because both have caused acute odor problems for surrounding communities

WHAT'S NEXT?

With its second phase recently launched, the landfill project is expected to raise the efficiency of methane recovery to 83% by 2012 compared to the 7% in 2003. eThekwini Municipality's work helped to explore the CDM pathway and prompted work on similar projects on the African continent in the near future.

COMPANIES INNOVATING TO CREATE A MORE SUSTAINABLE WORLD

Fuel-Efficient Driving in Real-Time

GPS software that provides real-time feedback on driving efficiency to save time and money while reducing fuel emissions

INNOVATION

GPS software that enables more efficient driving based on data from individual driving habits and specific routes

Collects and analyzes data on fuel consumption, local gas prices, driving style, number of stops, speed limits, and more, to calculate and show fuel carbon footprint and performance in one easy-to-read screen

SUSTAINABILITY

Real-time, on-route information facilitates smarter (green) driving

Users can track travel costs or plan future trips to find the most optimal route to reduce fuel emissions and save money

RESULTS

ecoRoute software is estimated to increase fuel efficiency beyond the 12% improvement when using traditional GPS systems

This translates to a decrease of at least 0.91 metric tons in carbon dioxide emissions per driver every year

DRIVERS

ECONOMIC DOWNTURN: The 2008 global economic downturn along with escalating concerns about the environment prompted investigating how to help drivers conserve both money and fuel

TARGET THE ELEPHANT: Road transport is by far the largest transport emission source and the global increase in passenger transport volume drastically increases greenhouse gas emissions

GREEN COMMITMENT: Garmin's ongoing commitment to creating environmentally conscious products with minimal environmental impact throughout their lifecycles

BARRIERS

TECHNOLOGY: An algorithm to handle the wide range of data available was difficult — it had to include data like driving habits, number of stops, distance, elevation changes, traffic, speed limits, weather and more

IMPATIENT CRITICS: Some critics contend that ecoRoute's "Less Fuel" option may come out with longer routes instead of faster alternatives, implying that Garmin's ecoRoute may save on gas, but not time

STIFF COMPETITION: The presence of other strong GPS systems poses a threat to user penetration of Garmin products and services

ENABLERS

PILOT PROJECT: Initial research in 2006 by University of Michigan students under the same project name, "ecoRoute," provided an early working model for the software

EMPOWERMENT: Users eager to reduce money spent on fuel can access comprehensive driving data to see how their habits impact travel expenses and drivers could make driving adjustments accordingly

FREE UPGRADE: Offering ecoRoute as a free software upgrade allowed existing users to adopt the system easily, making Garmin more attractive to both existing and potential buyers

IMPACT

SMARTER CAR DRIVERS: Useful information, such as the cost for a "one-way trip to the office," helps subscribers see travel costs to minimize personal and business travel expenses

GREENER BRAND: The software allowed Garmin to strengthen its brand among consumers concerned about driving greener and saving resources

PERSONAL SAVINGS: The money users save on fuel may now be allotted to other personal needs

WHAT'S NEXT?

Garmin is set to offer software that can collect data directly from individual cars, consolidating real-time information from an on-board diagnostic system that connects customizable gauges and monitoring utilities to the car's GPS.

Eco-Friendly Mini-Factory for Food

A small capacity yogurt factory built to address malnourishment and poverty using sustainable local resources and a novel business model

INNOVATION

Grameen Bank and Groupe Danone have partnered to develop a self-sustaining enterprise business that produces fortified yogurt for the local community using only local resources and sales and distribution capabilities in Bogra, Bangladesh

SUSTAINABILITY

The factory uses renewable resources such as solar energy and rainwater recycling

Yogurt is packaged in biodegradable cups made from cornstarch

RESULTS

The factory produces 22,000 pounds daily, enough to provide breakfast for 130,000 children; the successful pilot is now being scaled up

Yogurt is priced as low as $0.09 per 2.1 ounce serving, making it affordable to the poorest people

DRIVERS

LEADER'S VISION: The CEOs of Grameen Bank in Bangladesh and Groupe Danone in France — Dr. Muhammad Yunus and Franck Riboud — joined efforts to maximize the positive social and green impact of their businesses

HIGH POVERTY: Bangladesh is one of the world's poorest countries with about 40% of the population living under the poverty level — many on less than $3 per day

MALNOURISHED CHILDREN: 54% of preschool-age children are stunted, 56% are underweight and 17% are on the verge of starvation — many also suffer from deficiencies of vitamin A, iron, iodine and zinc

BARRIERS

MILK SUPPLY: The location of farmers in remote areas combined with the absence of refrigerated trucks often made transporting milk to traditional processing factories time-consuming and impractical

LACK OF INFRASTRUCTURE: Danone's distribution system, which employs refrigerated trucks and air-conditioned warehouses common in developed countries, was not suitable for Bangladesh

CHILDREN DISLIKE PRODUCT: The new yogurt "Shokti Doi" was fortified with Vitamin A, iron, calcium, zinc, protein and iodine, but the first samples were rejected by children because it was too runny and not sweet enough

ENABLERS

COMMITTED PARTNERS: Working with the International Cooperative Alliance (ICA) from Switzerland, Grameen Danone identified an enzyme used in Brazil which could preserve milk during the required transport time

NEW DISTRIBUTION MODEL: The company uses door-to-door sales by the "Grameen Ladies" – micro-entrepreneurs selling yogurt from the mini-factory to Bogra and surrounding villages

INVOLVE THE CONSUMERS: Danone experts improved yogurt with syrup made from locally grown date palms, a traditional sweetener, and refined the level of sweetness by using taste trials

IMPACT

INTERNAL: Exploiting this new production, supply and distribution model, Grameen Danone has launched new products and doubled its annual sales during its first three years

EMPLOYMENT OPPORTUNITIES: The company provides jobs to the local community — the door-to-door selling model employs about 500 women and about 50 factory workers

IMPROVED NUTRITION: One container of the yogurt provides 30% of a child's daily requirement of vitamins, iron, zinc and iodine

WHAT'S NEXT?

After the initial success in Bogra, Grameen Danone Foods Ltd. plans to build 50 mini-factories by 2020, each with an annual production capacity of 3,000 tons, thus meeting the needs of 150 million people.

Farmer Field Schools in Rural Asia

Sustainable cotton cultivation that creates a win-win-win for the private sector, NGOs and rural farmers through in-country pilot projects

INNOVATION
Use discovery-based learning (instead of charitable donations or regulatory measures) to persuade rural Indian and Pakistani farmers that using less water and pesticide, more effectively, improves their bottom line

SUSTAINABILITY
The program trains farmers on how to use chemicals and water in ways that are safer for people and the environment and that improve a farmer's financial return, increasing the likelihood that these practices gain wider acceptance

RESULTS
In Pakistani pilot projects, the average use of pesticides dropped 48%, the use of fertilizers by 32% and water use by 40%

At the same time, farmers' earnings increased by 87%

DRIVERS

HIGH NO$_2$ EMISSIONS: The inefficient overuse of pesticides and fertilizers has harmful effects on both people and the environment

WATER POLLUTION: The Indus River is threatened by pollution and intensive water extraction

WATER EFFICIENCY: While 90% of water taken from the Indus is used in agriculture, only 30% actually reaches crops while water availability is in rapid decline

KEY RESOURCES: As cotton is one of IKEA's most important raw materials sourced from Pakistan and India, the company is directly affected by the problem

BARRIERS

LACK OF EXPERIENCE: As a profit-oriented company, IKEA did not have the skills and resources of a non-profit organization, which are needed to cope with social and infrastructure challenges

RESISTANCE TO CHANGE: It is hard to convince farmers to change their practices, since small-scale growers are risk-averse

CHILD LABOR: Responsible companies have to deal with the additional problem of child labor, which is widespread in the cotton-seed-producing areas

ENABLERS

COMMITTED PARTNERS: A partnership was founded on IKEA's and the World Wildlife Fund's unique competencies — and involvement of local farmer organizations was crucial to be effective

PILOT PROJECTS: Discovery-based learning with farmers, demonstration plots and the success of participating farmers provided inspiration for thousands in the region

CHILDREN'S RIGHTS: Since 2005, IKEA's Social Initiative has supported UNICEF's children's rights programs in India — the aim is to create a protective environment for children in more than 1,847 villages

IMPACT

ENVIRONMENT: In Pakistani pilot projects, the average use of pesticides has dropped 48%, the use of fertilizers has decreased by 32% and water use by 40%

HEALTH: Decreasing pollution and better use of chemicals have a positive effect on the population's health

FARMERS' INCOME: Thanks to increasing efficiency and decreasing use of chemicals, farmers' earnings have increased by 87%

INTERNAL: With its involvement, IKEA found a way to make its business sustainable while improving the livelihood and health of farmers

WHAT'S NEXT?

Both IKEA and World Wildlife Fund acknowledge that making lasting change will require persistence, so they will continue the project in Pakistan and India. IKEA plans to extend this partnership to similar projects in Poland, China, Sweden and the United Kingdom.

Vélib' Bicycle Rental Program

Private-public partnership provides bikes anywhere in Paris to reduce the need for intracity vehicle travel

INNOVATION
The Vélib' program by the City of Paris and JCDecaux provides a bicycle-for-rent service that is integrated into the city's public transport system and offers low cost bicycle renting (free for the first half hour) at 1,451 stations across Paris

SUSTAINABILITY
Vélib' reduces the use of cars for short trips inside the city, thereby diminishing traffic congestion, noise pollution and air pollution

RESULTS
In the first three months of operation in 2007 there were 100,000 users daily, reducing CO_2 emissions by 32,330 tons annually — Paris will also generate an estimated €34M over the first 10 years without any investment

DRIVERS

CITY'S COMMITMENT: Paris's Mobility Plan and Climate Plan of 2007 aimed for a 75% reduction in greenhouse gas emissions by 2050 from 2004 levels

SIMILAR PROJECTS: Similar programs were successful in Lyon, Barcelona, Stockholm and other European cities

LEADER'S VISION: The initiative was championed by Paris mayor, Bertrand Delanoë, from the French Socialist Party

HEAVY TRAFFIC: Paris suffers from daily traffic jams and city car use is still increasing — bicycles as an eco-friendly alternative became more popular

BARRIERS

LACK OF EXPERIENCE: The city council did not have the experience to implement a bicycle renting system and other cities' failed attempts suggested high risk

VANDALISM & THEFT: These are common set-backs faced by public bike systems, which were the greatest problems faced by JCDecaux's pilot projects as well

CUSTOMER NEGLECT: Similar projects faced high maintenance and replacement costs because riders of public bikes often neglected caring for them

PRICING STRATEGY: Previous pricing strategies often resulted in decreasing availability — low prices encouraged riders to keep bikes for an entire day while high prices decreased use

ENABLERS

PARTNERSHIP: Paris formed a public-private partnership with JCDecaux, an advertising company that had already implemented a similar project in Vienna

REGISTRATION: Vandalism problems were addressed by making registration with a credit card mandatory, which transferred responsibility for the bike to the user

DURABLE BIKES: To increase endurance, the bikes are made of unique, durable parts, such as solid rubber tires — they are also equipped with a locking system

BUSINESS MODEL: In order to encourage people to make short rentals, a progressive cost-structure program was put in place — only the first half-hour is free

IMPACT

ENVIRONMENT: By lowering auto traffic, the program generated an estimated reduction of 32,330 tons of CO_2 emissions annually

CITY OF PARIS: JCDecaux invested €80 million upfront, will pay operating costs plus €3.4 million annually to Paris for rights to advertising space on 1,600 billboards

INTERNAL: JCDecaux expects to generate around €60 million annually in advertising revenues

COMMUNITY: Citizens and tourists got a cheap alternative to public transportation and cars, and at the same time Paris became cleaner and less noisy

WHAT'S NEXT?

Vélib' became the largest successful program of its kind in the world and serves as a good example for other urban areas. Because of continuing high demand, Vélib' will be extended to 29 towns on outskirts of Paris.

Power Plastic® Flexible Solar Cells

Off-grid solar power solution with a flexible form-factor that can be customized for a range of applications

INNOVATION

- Flexible, shapeable solar cells made of plastic instead of ceramic
- High-speed, low-cost production with continuous printing versus batch processing
- Form-factor opens a range of new uses from building structures to electronics to clothing

SUSTAINABILITY

- Collects renewable energy from the sun
- Cost, toxicity and availability of starting materials is lower than that used for silicon-based cells
- Production process uses lower temperature and is less energy intensive

RESULT

- Konarka's Power Plastic is opening new applications like stationary umbrellas that provide shade and power for personal electronics
- Some companies are looking at this technology to create construction materials

DRIVERS

TECHNOLOGY PUSH: A group of research scientists from UMass Lowell and other institutions made a critical technology discovery related to producing low-cost, flexible solar cell materials

CUT MY COSTS: Existing solar cells were cost-prohibitive, time consuming and rigid, limiting their application beyond traditional large-scale solar arrays or specific applications where off-grid solar power was the only solution

DEMAND PULL: The US military's increased usage of electronic devices and the desire to use these technologies in remote regions has driven the search for portable, safe, and durable energy sources

BARRIERS

LACK OF EXPERIENCE: The scientists involved in the discovery formed Konarka to further develop the technology; however, as material scientists, their experience had been focused on pure research

SACRIFICE NOTHING: Konarka's solar cells did not have the same lifespan or energy conversion properties as traditional solar cells — potential customers would not be interested unless there were improvements

PRODUCTION LIMITATIONS: While the discovery proved that solar cells could be printed on flexible, low-cost materials, it required a proprietary printing process that kept costs above acceptable levels

ENABLERS

INCUBATION: UMass Lowell provided critical upfront support to Konarka with IP licensing, labs and equipment, scientists, leadership coaching, and seed funding in exchange for a stake in the company

RESOURCES AND TALENT: The firm raised over $170 million to attract leading scientists and executives with relevant industry experience to support the rapid development and production of more advanced flexible solar cells

DON'T REINVENT THE WHEEL: Konarka combined its IP with existing assets to reduce costs and speed up production — it repurposed existing inkjet technology, purchased a closed Polaroid plant and hired former plant managers

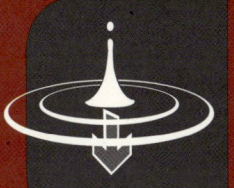

IMPACT

UNIVERSITY: Close ties with UMass Lowell allowed many students to take part in and learn from Konarka's research; the company is cited as one of the most successful examples of the university incubator program

INDUSTRY: Konarka created a new market for its coatable, flexible, plastic cells which can be used in a wide range of applications never before considered and where traditional solar cells are unable to compete

CUSTOMERS: The company announced that it will begin shipping its lightweight and mobile solar cells for use in "off-grid" applications including tents, backpacks and battery chargers

WHAT'S NEXT?

Although the initial application of Konarka's technology was modest, recent partnerships are a strong indicator of future potential. In May 2009, Konarka and Arch Aluminum & Glass signed an agreement to develop and produce building-integrated photovoltaics — solar cells embedded into building materials!

Beyond Smart Meters to Smart Grids

Malta's nationwide smart grid will transform how the country uses its limited resources and will create models for smart grid rollout around the world

INNOVATION

Malta has used creative partnerships to address dependency on imported fossil fuels and energy intensive desalination

Brings together EU funding, smart meters from ENEL, software solutions from IBM, and new integrated network management from ABB

SUSTAINABILITY

The smart grid enables Malta's utilities to better manage their systems

By understanding where, when and how electricity and water are used, the island will identify loss points and reduce over-production

RESULTS

About $100M has already been invested by the Malta Water and Power Utilities

The network should be completed by 2012 replacing all 250,000 analog electricity meters with new smart electronic devices

DRIVERS

UNACCEPTABLE WASTE: The cost of fossil fuels for electric power generation as well as desalination created a strong government will to reduce water and power waste, ranging as high as 40 to 70 percent around the world

GOVERNMENT INITIATIVES: Maltese government had been trying to encourage conservation in both water and power use for years — recent increases in costs and public awareness about the complexity of solution added momentum

TECHNOLOGY SUPPLIER PUSH: Technology leaders have pushed for the adoption of smarter water and power management for years and began to work together to provide more momentum for the push into smart grids

BARRIERS

HIGH COST AND COMPLEXITY: Each of the critical pieces of the solution has a substantial price tag and can be very costly to implement and manage given the many players involved on both the supplier and user side

ANTIQUATED SYSTEMS: Both physical and management systems are antiquated in most parts of the developed world with large amounts of both water and power losses in the distribution systems and waste on the customer side

MULTIPLE PLAYERS & UTILITIES: The situation in Malta and most other developed areas is complicated by multiple overlapping utilities and levels of government

ENABLERS

EU FUNDING AND INCENTIVES: As in most other demonstration areas in Europe and North America, it has taken extra funding and support from higher levels of government to get rapid movement — in this case it was the EU

ENABLING TECHNOLOGIES: The combination of smart digital meters for both water and power as well as supporting management technologies and systems was seen as enabling major improvements in antiquated systems

PUBLIC-PRIVATE PARTNERS: IBM along with other industry players has entered into a partnership with Malta to install 250,000 smart meters throughout the island — the system will allow customers to monitor their energy use

IMPACT

GOVERNMENT EFFICIENCY: While the impact has mainly resulted in improved efficiency of systems development, acquisition, and installation, it is hoped that improved operations management of the infrastructure will soon follow

PROMISE OF EFFICIENT USE: The major promises of smart grids lie in lower costs and environmental impact associated with meeting increasing demands with current facilities and in the much more efficient use of power an water

INDUSTRY PARTNERSHIPS: The partnerships that have come together for smart grid demonstrations are enabling more efficient development and implementation of complete solutions that would have been difficult for single entities

WHAT'S NEXT?

The success of major smart grid demonstration in places like Malta, Boulder (Colorado), northern California and Hawaii will be a major factor in increasing the effectiveness of the technologies and systems as well as our understanding of what it will take to significantly improve the efficiency of both power and water use and management.

Abu Dhabi's City-size Bet on Green

A planned city for fifty thousand residents designed to be carbon neutral is emerging as a global hub for green technology

INNOVATION
The mandate to be carbon neutral and emission free combined with immense sovereign wealth and public-private partnerships are motivating innovators from around the world to set up their operations in Abu Dhabi's carbon neutral development project

SUSTAINABILITY
New systems, processes, and technologies to reduce or remove environmental impact have been developed (or are in progress) across all aspects of city life—from transportation to energy to building construction

RESULTS
$15 billion will be invested through 2020 towards the growth of the renewable energy market and other global energy solutions

New, more efficient technologies are emerging each year

DRIVERS

VAST, BUT LIMITED OIL: Abu Dhabi has almost 10% of the world's oil; however, most reserves (including Abu Dhabi's) are forecasted to run out in the next 50-75 years

TACKLE THE ELEPHANTS: As part of the UAE, Abu Dhabi has the largest per capita carbon footprint in the world — radical solutions would be needed

LEADERSHIP: Abu Dhabi's rulers and the appointed CEO of Masdar recognized the city's competitiveness required a shift from being an oil exporter to an *energy* exporter

PATIENT CAPITAL: Abu Dhabi committed $15 billion dollars to get the Masdar city initiative up and running

BARRIERS

STATUS QUO: As a city with little public transportation and extremely cheap fossil fuels (e.g., $0.45/gallon gas), there was not a pressing reason to change

LOW SKILL LEVELS: The city and its economy would be based on thousands of skilled workers and inhabitants, but less than 15% of the city's citizens go on to college

HARSH ENVIRONMENT: With temps that rise to 125°F and little fresh water, achieving a zero waste and carbon neutral city required new technologies, processes and systems

LOCATION: In addition to the extreme environment, Abu Dhabi is a relatively remote location not known for green research — attracting companies proved difficult

ENABLERS

INWARD + OUTWARD: Masdar is investing in local projects and initiatives around the world to establish itself and the new city as a leader in field

PARTNERSHIPS: Masdar partnered with some of the world's best scientists, firms and institutions to set up shop in Masdar — MIT is building a campus in the city

PROTOTYPES: New technologies are being piloted in the city — in 2010, Bayer MaterialScience agreed to build and test an ultra efficient building design

GOVERNMENT INCENTIVES: Abu Dhabi located Masdar close to the international airport and created a free zone in Masdar, offering 100% business ownership, tax breaks, and IP rights

IMPACT

FORCING EFFECT: Masdar's size is pushing suppliers towards cleaner solutions — aluminum producers created a product that "cost" 90% fewer emissions to produce

EXPANDING MANDATE: The Masdar group has expanded into other green areas including a project to develop carbon credits from emissions-reducing projects in Africa and Asia

EMERGING SUSTAINABILITY HUB: In 2009, over 50 renewable energy businesses started operations in Masdar with up to 70 more planned for 2010; additionally, the World Future Energy Summit is sponsored by Masdar — cleantech innovation prizes worth 10 times more than similar events outside the UAE are attracting more and more investors and firms to Masdar

WHAT'S NEXT?

Masdar expects to contribute 7% of the energy needs of the Emirates by 2020 with new developments in the renewable energy market to be valued at around $6-8 billion.

All-Electric Commercial Vehicles

The first commercial, zero-emission electric van that is "battery-agnostic" has gained approval across the European Union

INNOVATION

Working within the limits of existing electric vehicle (EV) technology, Modec's commercial van is purpose-built for delivery vans used within a defined radius

Its "future-proof" battery compartment allows Modec to use different batteries as technologies evolve

SUSTAINABILITY

The electric van has zero carbon emissions and is virtually silent while also completely comparable in economy and performance to diesel equivalents

Partnering with Navistar in the US will enable Modec to significantly impact air quality and CO_2 emissions in urban areas in North America

RESULTS

Each e-van is estimated to save more than 9 tons of CO_2 per year

Over 150 vehicles have been built since production began in 2007 and the company expects to ramp up to 400+ vehicles per year in the future

DRIVERS

LEADER'S VISION: Modec's founder saw the need for alternatives to the combustion engine — he was an early adopter of the Prius, but wanted a 100% electric vehicle

TAX POLICY: Large cities such as London and many others in Europe and the US have instituted fees to tax emissions and encourage zero-emission vehicles

A CURRENT NEED: Existing batteries limited EVs to small two-seaters with low ranges — more sizeable vehicles require much larger batteries which only vans can hold

GROWING MARKET: About 320,000 vans are sold annually in the UK, and the market is growing rapidly due to the increase in online shopping

BARRIERS

EVOLVING TECH: Changing battery technologies and costs make it very difficult to freeze the design of cost competitive e-vehicles

LOW VOLUMES: Commercial vans are generally produced in low volumes and the costs of newly designed assembly lines have been a barrier to new breakthrough vehicles

WORKER RESISTANCE: Managers of delivery fleets were resistant to major changes in vehicles and the new van's competitiveness vs. diesel vans was met with skepticism

PARTS AVAILABILITY: Securing sufficient batteries and appropriate software forced a slow-down in production in the first year

ENABLERS

MODULAR DESIGN: Purpose-designed vans allow for various charging options, making them "future proof" and allowing use of evolving battery capacities and chemistries

LOWER COMPLEXITY: A far simpler electric engine and drive components with fewer moving parts lowers production costs even for small volume production

LEAD CUSTOMERS: Modec secured customers with large fleets of delivery vehicles including TESCO, FedEx, UPS, and others who benefit from the cost effectiveness and PR value

NEW BUSINESS MODEL: Battery costs are not included in the price of the vehicle — they are leased from GE Capital, lowering upfront costs and increasing market potential

IMPACT

INDUSTRY: The success of Modec's e-vans in lead markets stimulated the development of a more reliable and advanced supplier base for electric vehicles

CUSTOMERS: Modec vans can travel up to 100 miles at a top speed of 50 mph carrying a load of two tons on one overnight charge

COST SAVINGS: Customers of fleet vehicles benefit from no road tax, no operator's license or road license — costs for maintenance are low

NEW MARKETS: With strong demand for the van, Modec has appointed distributors across Europe including the Netherlands, Ireland, France, Spain and Denmark

WHAT'S NEXT?

Modec recently entered into a JV with Navistar, the largest truck manufacturer in the US, to expand into the North American market and to establish a more reliable funding base for ongoing R&D and electric vehicle development.

Printing Process for Solar Cells

A revolutionary solar panel technology that delivers significant cost savings relative to conventional thin film solar panels

INNOVATION
Breakthrough printing process for thin-film solar cells that can replace expensive vacuum deposition and sputtering processes, resulting in very low-cost thin film solar panels

Nano-particle technology allows solar panels to be "printed" similar to a newspaper printing press

SUSTAINABILITY
High material utilization combined with low-energy processes dramatically shorten payback periods for solar cells to less than a year

RESULTS
Nanosolar has large scale production facilities operating in Germany (with 640 MW capacity) and in California (with 430 MW capacity)

Nanosolar Utility Panel™ cuts the per watt cost of solar panels to as little as $1, 1/5 the cost of silicon panels

DRIVERS

TACKLE THE ELEPHANT: Global warming and sustained oil prices of $70-90 per barrel are raising demand for alternative energy solutions

HIGH COSTS: The high price of silicon along with costly processes like sputtering and vacuum deposition make it quite expensive to produce silicon solar panels

LEADERS' VISION: Founders Martin Roscheisen and Brian Sager started the company with the vision of applying a "technologically aggressive approach to solar power"

DEMAND PULL: Spectacular growth is seen in thin-film solar cells — its market share is expected to grow from 8% in 2008 to 20% in 2010

BARRIERS

UNPROVEN TECHNOLOGY: Nanosolar needs to prove to customers that its technology works as efficiently and as reliably as traditional silicon panels

COSTLY ALTERNATIVE: Solar power has been too costly to be accepted widely as an alternative — even the cheapest solar panels cost $3 per watt while coal produces energy at $1

TECHNOLOGY: Thin-film solar cells face technology challenges to overcome the slow and expensive vacuum process for semiconductor deposition

RAISING CAPITAL: Materials-based businesses require a longer-than-average time for ROI, which discourages some investors

ENABLERS

CONVERSION RATE: The US Dept. of Energy has verified thermal conversion efficiency of over 16% for individual Nanosolar films, which is almost double that of other thin film solar cells

COST REDUCTION: Nanosolar cells use no silicon; they also save up to 40% on mounting and cabling materials and labor compared to silicon cells

NEW TECHNIQUE: Nanosolar has moved the manufacturing model from one that looks like semiconductor wafer production to one that looks like printing

AVAILABLE FUNDING: Nanosolar has attracted the largest amount of venture financing of any private company during Q2 2006 and during Q1 2008 — total of $500M

IMPACT

INDUSTRY STRUCTURE: With equivalent thermal efficiencies and significantly lower costs than silicon, thin film solar producers will likely increase their current 20% market share

INDUSTRY CAPACITY: Nanosolar has increased manufacturing capacity in the US and Europe with reported solar cell costs of $.36 per watt and panel costs less than $1 per watt

POWER OUTPUT: Power output ranges from 160W to 220W, which is approximately three times more power per panel than conventional thin-film panel

CUSTOMERS: Nanosolar Utility Panel™ is the first solar panel certified by TÜV for a system voltage of 1500V, or 50% higher than current standards

WHAT'S NEXT?

The pace of technology improvements in solar is likely to continue to increase, thus enabling a significant increase in solar's share of total energy production and Nanosolar's potential.

COMPANIES INNOVATING TO CREATE A MORE SUSTAINABLE WORLD

Brazilian Biodiversity for Cosmetics

Capturing the essence of Natura's commitment to personal, social and environmental well-being in cosmetics sourced ethically from the rainforest

INNOVATION

Ekos lines of cosmetics focus on the sustainable use of raw materials drawn from value chain partnerships in Brazil's biodiverse rainforest

The concept uniquely taps into local and international passions for Brazil, its rain forest and sustainability

SUSTAINABILITY

Natura ensures that ingredients are sustainably farmed and farmers are fairly compensated

In addition, Ekos uses packaging that can be easily refilled with specially designed refill solutions

RESULTS

Sales of the Ekos line have grown substantially to become one of Natura's major product lines, enabling the firm to sustain 15-20% growth and a brand value to more than 133% of sales

DRIVERS

LEADER'S VISION: "We don't include environment in our strategy, it is our strategy" and has been consistently since the company was founded in 1969

COMPANY CULTURE: The entire organization passionately lives the company's principles that include minimizing environmental impact and promoting sustainability

DIFFERENT IS GOOD: Recognizing it could not compete with the large budgets of multinational cosmetics firms, Natura wanted to be distinct and draw on its Brazilian roots

ACQUISITION: In 1999, Natura bought Flora Medicinal, a company focused on the use of extracts from natural origin as medicines or health-promoting agents

BARRIERS

NATURAL ISN'T EASY: Difficult to be 100% natural given shelf life requirements and the fact that some cosmetics like hair dyes and nail polish are inherently damaging

RAPID GROWTH: While rapid growth is an objective, it is also difficult to achieve while staying carbon neutral and true to the strong environmentally based culture

WEAK SUPPLY CHAIN: Needed infrastructure and farming practices to support sustained supply from the Amazon regions weren't really in place

INTEGRATION ISSUES: Natura primarily focused on organic growth and the acquisition was not as successful as had been hoped

ENABLERS

SUSTAINABILTY CHOICE: R&D and partners enabled the company to launch Ekos and replace mineral/petroleum/animal-based ingredients with sustainable plant-based products

SALES CONSULTANTS: With over 1M active sales consultants, Natura uses strong training/relationship programs that enable rapid customer feedback and innovation support

PROJECTS & PARTNERS: Funded development projects and training in sustainable production led to the establishment of certification guidelines to support the needed supply

UNUSED ASSETS: Despite the poor integration, Natura was able to make significant use of Flora's R&D initiatives into Brazilian biodiversity

IMPACT

PROFITABLE GROWTH: Ekos has enjoyed double-digit growth, strong profitability and has won many sustainability awards, availing it strong brand position and leadership

EMPLOYEES: Natura is now one of the most desired places to work in the region and was recently chosen as one of the best producers of leadership talent globally

VALUE CHAIN: Supplier partnerships with numerous agricultural communities that include reserves from the sales of products using their ingredients

INTERNAL: Natura has one of the largest R&D operations of any South American-based firm and is a leading innovator in products, sustainability and business models

WHAT'S NEXT?

Natura continues to expand the sustainable plant-based ingredients in its Ekos line and is gaining share and scaling up across Latin America and Europe. It is also extending greenovations into other product lines and customer segments.

Plant-based Plastics

More than 50% lower carbon footprint bioplastics made from corn sugar with performance and cost comparable to traditional plastics

INNOVATION
NatureWorks' Ingeo is the first commercially available plastic made from corn sugar — it is 1/200th the cost of earlier bio-plastics and is competitive with petroleum-based traditional plastics in terms of cost and performance

SUSTAINABILITY
These bioplastics are produced using significantly less energy than traditional plastics and have a wide variety of end-of-life options, including recycling, composting and incinerating

RESULTS
The new manufacturing process lowers carbon dioxide emissions by 60% and reduces energy needed by 35%

Bioplastics also have the potential to reduce landfill waste

DRIVERS

GROWTH FROM INNOVATION: Changes in the food industry including decreasing margins in commodities prompted Cargill to look for new areas of growth for the company — from trading corn to making plastics from it

EXPENSIVE INPUTS: Higher and more volatile oil prices have increased the attractiveness of corn plastics as an alternative to petroleum-based plastics

TECHNOLOGY PUSH: Corn plastics have been around for 20 years but were too expensive to make — Patrick Gruber, a Cargill chemist, invented a way to make the plastics more efficiently at 1/200th the original cost

BARRIERS

LACK OF EXPERIENCE: Cargill had the technology and the manufacturing expertise to produce bioplastics but lacked the network and experience to bring the product to the market

ESTABLISHED STAKEHOLDERS: Recyclers of petroleum-based plastic bottles are resistant to the commercialization of bioplastics because it can act as a contaminant when mixed with petroleum-based plastics

LACK OF SUPPORT SYSTEMS: Some disposal choices for Ingeo bioplastics — recycling, industrial composting, incinerating — are neither commercially viable nor readily accessible at present

ENABLERS

COMMITTED PARTNERS: Cargill formed a 50-50 joint venture with Teijin Limited to form NatureWorks — Teijin's expertise on fibers, films and plastics will facilitate product expansion and its global network will help accelerate sales

FILLING THE VOID: The company instituted a buy-back program to collect post-consumer bioplastics from recycling facilities and route them to the appropriate end-of-life solution based on geographic location

NEW RESEARCH: NatureWorks has been able to pilot the use of hydrolysis to chemically recycle its bioplastics — successfully commercializing this method will make the use of bioplastics a true cradle-to-cradle system

IMPACT

INTERNAL: Due to expected sales growth of 10-20% in 2009, NatureWorks has formed new partnerships in South America and has doubled their manufacturing capacity to 300 million pounds

CUSTOMERS: Customers such as Walmart, Wild Oats, KLM Airlines, Marks & Spencer and Newman's Own Organics have started using bioplastics as cups, bottles or food containers to boost their visibility in sustainability

COMPETITORS: Other companies such as Mirel and NEC have formed partnerships to produce and commercialize bioplastics and are now engaged in research and collaborative efforts to achieve the goal of zero waste

WHAT'S NEXT?

In July 2009, Cargill acquired full ownership of NatureWorks LLC. Cargill is now working with several other companies to create the required separating and recycling infrastructure for a fully recyclable product.

A Precise Water Delivery System

An irrigation method that reduces water loss and use of fertilizer in agriculture by changing the way water is applied to the soil

INNOVATION
Drip irrigation reduces the use of water and fertilizer employed in farming by allowing water to drip slowly into the soil—a major improvement over spray or flood irrigation which use much more water than needed by the plants

SUSTAINABILITY
This method increases the efficiency of water use in agriculture, allows for reuse of recycled water, decreases use of fertilizer and prevents soil erosion

RESULTS
Netafim, which pioneered drip irrigation in 1965, is now a global leader in irrigation solutions

The method can reduce water use by 40% and increase mineral efficiency by 20% vs. conventional methods

DRIVERS

EUREKA MOMENT: Simcha Blass, an Israeli water engineer, saw the potential of drip irrigation when, by chance, a farmer showed him a tree that grew because of a leaking pipe when other trees around it did not

DREAMS OF HOMELAND: Blass was born and raised in Poland but he started developing inventions such as a wheat planting machine and aqueducts with the aim of enabling and improving farming in Israel

WATER SHORTAGE: The Hatzerim Kibbutz, one of the many agricultural communities that settled Israel, realized they could never survive on agriculture alone in the desert and began searching for ways to diversify

BARRIERS

BUSINESS RESOURCES: Blass and his son Yeshayahu continued to work on developing the first modern drip irrigation system but lacked the resources to commercialize their invention

MATERIAL LIMITATION: The traditional components in drip irrigation were clay pipes, perforated pipes or porous canvas hoses, but water released through tiny holes in these pipes were easily blocked by tiny particles

OPENNESS: Because the community did not prioritize protecting its innovations from outsiders, their technology was open to rivals from all over Israel and the world

ENABLERS

COMMITTED PARTNERS: Blass partnered with a kibbutz—an agricultural community with manufacturing capabilities, experience and networks—to form Netafim and to bring the product to market

IMPROVING TECHNOLOGY: The advent of modern plastics during and after World War II made it possible to combine plastic tubing and emitters to make larger and longer passageways that could release water slowly

BUSINESS MODEL: By providing a complete service from installation to maintenance, focusing only on agriculture-related business and demonstrating fiscal responsibility, Netafim was able to grow and lead their market

IMPACT

COMMUNITY: Netafim was able to provide income and jobs to kibbutz or community members including benefits such as health insurance, homes, cars and education of their children even if they left the kibbutz

FOOD AND WATER SUPPLY: Drip irrigation has taken on an increased importance throughout the world, particularly in high-risk poverty and desert areas that need to increase crop yield and to conserve scarce water supplies

GLOBAL PRESENCE: Netafim has sales of over $600 million and a presence in 110 countries across five continents

WHAT'S NEXT?

Netafim has continued to expand globally with new projects including building the largest drip irrigation system for sugar cane cultivation in Brazil and constructing another system in Peru for converting sugar cane to ethanol.

COMPANIES INNOVATING TO CREATE A MORE SUSTAINABLE WORLD

Resource Usage Feedback System

Communicating personal usage patterns changes individual behavior and improves overall resource utilization

INNOVATION
Real-time monitoring and communication of individual energy use within Oberlin College buildings

Combined with a college-wide student competition to publish results and increase motivation

SUSTAINABILITY
Create awareness of individual and community usage and wastage of energy while modifying behavior to use resources more effectively

IMPACT
32% decrease in electricity use and 3% decrease in water use during competition period

Follow-up student surveys indicate long-term benefits of students continuing to manage building resources carefully

DRIVERS

LEADER'S VISION: Demonstrate concern for, and protection of, Oberlin's physical environment through its own actions and education

TACKLE THE ELEPHANT: Over 90% of Oberlin's resource use occurs inside buildings

STAKEHOLDER DEMAND: Oberlin attracts a progressive student body that is passionate and committed to initiatives that support the environment

BARRIERS

NO FINANCIAL INCENTIVE: All dorm residents pay the same Room & Board fees regardless of resource use — no individual financial incentive to reduce usage

UPFRONT COSTS: Like other campuses, Oberlin's buildings were built over an extended time with most buildings 10 years or older — retrofitting initiatives or smart appliance installations were too expensive

TRAGEDY OF THE COMMONS: Traditional water or electric meters report usage for the whole building — individuals did not feel their individual usage made a difference in the big picture

ENABLERS

CROSS-FUNCTIONAL TEAM: Oberlin developed and executed the project with internal resources to lower costs using research done by professors, software and program management by IT staff and students from different disciplines

RESULTS-BASED INVESTMENT: The project used a phased approach to prove and implement the concept; this attracted investments from the US EPA and DOE, Ohio Dept. of Development, and US Green Building Council

EXISTING TECHNOLOGIES: Technology for data acquisition, processing and displaying was created by combining off-the-shelf sensors, inexpensive wireless logging and networking hardware with a web-based dashboard

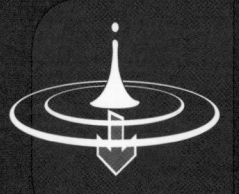

IMPACT

CUSTOMERS: The program is an example of Oberlin "walking-the-talk" of a sustainable campus raising awareness of responsible resource use with students and teachers, today and tomorrow

PARTNERS: The project proved the concept and enabled investors and observers to use the technologies, programs and project learning to roll-out feedback systems in other settings across the country

COMPETITORS: In 2005, Oberlin won a national student design competition for sustainability run by the US EPA, creating interest and awareness of Oberlin's commitment to sustainability

WHAT'S NEXT?

A post-competition study concluded that the feedback system created substantial short-term reductions in resource use and had the potential to create long-term behavioral changes: tenants teach themselves to conserve energy, which can be an effective alternative to existing "smart building" control technology.

Sustainable Agriculture in Nigeria

Creating win-win value chains: Prosperity for farmers and profits for shareholders

INNOVATION

Olam has integrated banks, input suppliers, and donors into an input supply chain that simultaneously increases the quality and volume of rice paddy supply while improving the prosperity and food-security of small-scale farmers in Nigeria

SUSTAINABILITY

Private firms provide sustainable support to small scale farmers and ensure market forces are respected. Donors continue to play a critical role in supporting farmers during their adoption of more modern inputs and practices. This coordinated intra-preneurial approach supports rapid expansion of the model

RESULTS

Since 2006, farmers engaged as growers for Olam have seen yields rise from 1.7 to 4.7 tons of rice paddy per hectare of land

After the first two years of external debt financing, farmers are able to self-finance operations

DRIVERS

FOOD SECURITY: A global food shortage beginning in 2007 led to rapid increases in commodity food prices — commercial food producers saw opportunities to profit because of increasing demand and increasing commodity prices

MAKING MARKETS: Olam recognized the growing demand for high quality imported rice in Nigeria — transitioning farmers to modern varietals and practices would allow the company to offer domestic alternatives to imported rice

ENVIRONMENTAL AWARENESS Increasing rice production by expanding traditional farming practices promotes deforestation and adds substantial land clearing costs. In contrast, Olam supports sustainable yield increases from existing land under cultivation

BARRIERS

ENABLING ENVIRONMENT: Nigeria constantly ranks as one of the more corrupt countries in the world, but successful coordination across the supply chain requires both transparency and rapid return on investment for all participants

FARMER COORDINATION: The average farmer in Nigeria controls less than 1 hectare of land, requiring massive coordination efforts to aggregate commercial volumes of paddy consistently

UNBANKED POPULATION: Only a small percentage of rice farmers currently engaged in Olam's out grower program had a bank account before the program began, but bank accounts are the key to efficient lending and payment systems

ENABLERS

MAJOR DOMESTIC DEMAND: Nigeria imports much of the rice that is domestically consumed — in general, rice has become a staple in the diet of all Nigerians, and growing middle class and urban populations are demanding higher quality rice

BANKS SEEK EXPANDED BASE: Banks in Nigeria are seeking to expand their customer base, especially into rural areas — while average deposits remain very low, rural entrepreneurs are an attractive segment for banks to serve

CREATIVE DONOR: USAID embraced sustainable private sector driven development: in 2007, the USAID MARKETS program was launched to support integrating small-scale farmers into commercial value chains

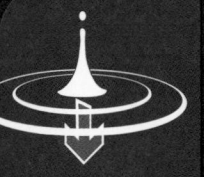

IMPACT

INCREASED YIELDS: Yields among participating farmers have nearly tripled, increasing the volume of paddy produced without clearing additional land — increased production density also eases collection logistics and costs

INCREASED PROFITS: Profits to participating farmers have more than doubled, making small-scale farming a viable business and leading to rapid expansion from fast-following farmers who see tangible rewards from current participants

FARMER SUSTAINABILITY: Farmers who reserve the increased profits from the sale of paddy can self-finance their seed and input purchasing in the second year — increased wealth is primarily spent in rural areas in local economy

WHAT'S NEXT?

Olam's success in rice is raising interest among other rice processors to engage in similar farmer support systems. Additionally, Olam is pursuing related activities in other commodity value chains, including sesame and cocoa.

COMPANIES INNOVATING TO CREATE A MORE SUSTAINABLE WORLD

Extremely Rugged Low Power Laptop

One Laptop Per Child has brought energy demands down to 2-3 watts, enabling a wide range of human and off-grid power sources

INNOVATION
One Laptop Per Child (OLPC) has designed, produced and delivered over 1.3 million XO laptops for under $200 each that require less than 2 watts of power for educational purposes in developing countries

SUSTAINABILITY
With power requirements of less than 1/10 than that required by conventional laptops, off-grid renewable and human power sources such as solar panels and human powered cranks can be used to run these computers

RESULTS
Every child in Uruguay primary schools now has an XO laptop, Peru and Rwanda are close behind, pushing other countries and companies to comparable solutions

DRIVERS

EDUCATIONAL MISSION: "Create educational opportunities for the world's poorest children, providing each with rugged, low-cost, low-power connected laptops with content and software designed for collaborative, joyful, self-empowered learning"

LEADER'S VISION: The passion of the designer, Nicholas Negroponte, MIT and its Media Lab, and of the OLPC Institute President and COO Chuck Kane have all been major drivers for the project

GOVERNMENT SUPPORT: Leaders in less developed areas are focused on education as the main platform to improve opportunity and quality of life and local educators are beginning to embrace technology

BARRIERS

SCARCE RESOURCES: The same children and communities that are so in need of education also have major needs for adequate food, water and health care, and have very limited resources

LIVING OFF-GRID: The same children and communities that do not have adequate education also do not have access to power grids and other resources while low-cost laptops still require 20-40 watts of power

STATUS QUO: Some teachers refused to use the laptops as an educational tool because they were unfamiliar with computers and the internet

ENABLERS

PUBLIC-PRIVATE PARTNERS: In addition to the partners required to produce and rollout the XO laptop, OLPC used partnerships to develop innovative power solutions including the Potenco yo-yo and solar cells

LOW COST CHILD-UP DESIGN: Low cost and low power design plus an extremely low cost supply chain met low cost targets — child-up rather than lab-down design philosophy drove user excitement

LOW POWER SOLUTIONS Designed to require less than 2 watts of power and enabled for multiple power sources and charging options, the XO has become the focus of a wide range of off-grid power solutions

IMPACT

LAPTOP INDUSTRY: By proving the feasibility and demand for a low cost educational laptop, OLPC has pushed the laptop industry in new directions and has raised manufacturers' awareness of the needs of developing countries

CHILDREN AND EDUCATORS: The XOs, their educational software and meshing capability have been very successful and have been embraced by both children and teachers as a collaborative learning tool

NATIONS: National leaders in countries such as Rwanda, Uruguay, and Peru have embraced OLPC as a win-win nation- and community-building tool, as have the World Bank and other NGOs

WHAT'S NEXT?

With over 1.3 million laptops distributed in Rwanda, Nigeria, Sri Lanka, Uruguay, Peru and other countries, OLPC is looking to scale up to 50 Million XOs so that other players will enter this market. Newer versions of the XO are intended to reach the elusive goal of $75-100 price and 1 watt of power consumption per device.

Standardized LED Systems for Cars

A simple, "plug and play," solution for vehicles that enables instant efficiency gains from LED lighting and can be easily customized to meet user needs

INNOVATION

A standardized approach to LED lighting for the auto industry

The JOULE™ product family is an easy to integrate, low cost lighting solution that fits within existing vehicle systems

SUSTAINABILITY

Uses 85% less energy than standard automotive lighting, and lasts the life of the vehicle

The efficiency gains and the associated fuel savings allow the system to pay for itself in less than three years

RESULTS

With over 1 million units sold, the product family has seen exponential growth since its launch in 2006. A vehicle's total carbon output can be reduced by 1-2% thanks to the improved fuel economy

DRIVERS

REGULATORY PUSH:
New emissions standards push the development of energy saving technologies. A European Union (EU) mandate requiring all vehicles sold there to have daytime running lamps by 2011

MARKET PULL:
Studies indicated that LED-powered daytime running lights can be 75% more efficient than the standard versions increased interest by OEMs motivated light system manufacturers to invest in LED R&D

TECHNOLOGY ADVANCEMENT:
The material chemistry and LED technology are developing rapidly. The amount of light that come out of an LED is twice or three times more than three years ago at the same power consumption

BARRIERS

TOTAL SYSTEM COSTS:
The average price of LED systems was too high because they were custom engineered for each and every vehicle. A new technology was needed to create an attractive alternative to older solutions

PERFORMANCE GAINS:
Migrating LED technology past brake lamps required dramatic gains in output to be feasible. The dedication of the company into fundamental R&D would be required

CHANGE PREFERENCE:
Car companies already understood the benefits of LEDs, but they still associated them with high total system cost and this had kept them from replacing the preferred old technologies

ENABLERS

NEW TECHNOLOGY:
The JOULE system by OSRAM allows total flexibility in design, in a standardized package. The package offers LED lighting without the complexity and cost of a custom LED assembly

SUPPORT TEAM &STRUCTURE:
Besides the corporate-wide collaboration, the most critical aspect has been staffing a respected optics and applications team to take the light sources and teach manufacturers how to use them in applications

REGULATORY REQUIREMENTS:
As more strict environmental come into effect, the push to adopt energy savings technologies becomes greater and greater. LEDs are an enabler to meeting these requirements

IMPACT

ENVIRONMENT:
OSRAM's JOULE system uses 85% less energy than a conventional lighting system which translates to a decreasing in total carbon output by 1-2% in the case of an all-LED lighting system

COMPANY:
OSRAM is on a trajectory for dramatic growth over the coming years. Efficiency gains will move LED lighting from signal applications to the predominant technology for headlamps and forward lighting.

INDUSTRY:
LEDs now dominate the tail and center-mounted brake light markets with a market share of 50% and a July 2009 Frost & Sullivan forecast estimates that number will jump to 80% by 2015

WHAT'S NEXT?

With the newest product in the JOULE platform the JFL2, OSRAM aims at the growing LED headlight market which is expected to reach 26% of the market by 2015

Common Threads Initiative

Design and manufacturing processes can include a viable zero-waste production and recycling process for clothing

INNOVATION
Thoughtful garment design enabled Patagonia to create a "closed-loop" process that ensures worn-out clothing is fully recyclable into new garments, whereas most performance clothing can be made from recycled material, but cannot be reused in similar garments

SUSTAINABILITY
Recycled polyester requires less energy to produce, resulting in lower costs and carbon emissions versus the traditional petroleum-based production process

The process also reduces landfill waste by recycling old clothing for new

RESULTS
On average, the process reduces energy use by 76% and CO_2 emissions by 42%

To date, Patagonia's Common Threads program has saved over 12,000kg of old clothing from landfills

DRIVERS

COMPANY CULTURE: Employee passion to live Patagonia's mission to "use business to inspire and implement solutions to the environmental crisis" motivated product managers to set an audacious goal for recyclability

LEAD CUSTOMERS: A core group of Patagonia customers ensures the company continues to assess its impact on the environment by critiquing manufacturing processes

MAINTAINING LEADERSHIP: As competitors duplicate Patagonia's previous greenovations, such as the use of recycled soda bottles in fleece, the company had to find new ways to differentiate and attract customers

BARRIERS

ENSURING TOTAL EFFICIENCY: The program had to maintain its ecological advantage over using petroleum feedstock while taking into account the carbon footprint required to ship used clothing to a partner based in Japan

MAINTAINING PERFORMANCE: Patagonia had to find a solution that balanced recyclability with garment performance because many materials that were easier to recycle did not meet minimum design requirements

EXISTING TECHNOLOGIES: Very few other firms are focused on recycling whole garments — once a garment is assembled, it's too complicated for most existing recycling systems to handle

ENABLERS

SENIOR SUPPORT: Founder and CEO Yvon Chouinard and the Board of Directors fully committed to developing a successful program that did not sacrifice performance or profitability

COMMITTED PARTNERS: TEIJIN Fibers, a long-term supplier, was able to develop a closed loop recycling system for polyester, a high performance material; Patagonia found other partners to process non-polyester clothing

SYSTEMS APPROACH: Patagonia's fabric development and clothing designers work with multiple suppliers and recycling partners to integrate recycled fabric and more easily recyclable designs without sacrificing quality

IMPACT

INDUSTRY: Patagonia has validated the concept of closed loop production systems as a viable model for garment manufacturing firms — the Clean Threads initiative helps firms with interests in creating such systems

CUSTOMERS: Patagonia has collected over 6,000 kilograms of garments — in 2009, around 80% of Patagonia apparel was recyclable through the Common Threads program

COMPETITORS: Others are following Patagonia's lead — MEC, a large Canadian outdoor store, introduced a garment recycling program two years after Patagonia that also accepts Common Threads branded clothing

WHAT'S NEXT?

Based on the positive customer response and commercial viability the company has announced its goal to make all of its products recyclable through the Common Threads program by 2010.

Shipping Containers as Shelters

Provides affordable alternatives to shanty towns by converting and upgrading shipping containers into sustainable, stackable housing

INNOVATION
PFNC transforms excess shipping containers into basic housing units — providing developed world amenities at emerging world prices

SUSTAINABILITY
Shipping containers in California are too expensive to recycle or ship empty back to China — but they can be inexpensively converted into transportable, semi-permanent housing units

Interiors use predominantly recycled materials

RESULT
The standardized, stackable homes sell for less than $8,000 and can become modules for larger buildings that form sustainable communities instead of temporary and unsafe shantytowns

DRIVERS

EXPLOSIVE GROWTH: Urban populations of developing regions are growing faster than the supply of homes

SAFETY: People in poor urban areas are forced to live in unsafe, substandard houses made from scrap building materials, creating a need for safer housing

LEADER'S VISION: On a trip to Juarez, Mexico, the founder was shocked to see people living in shanty-towns even though the economy was growing rapidly through substantial investment by large US manufacturing firms

BARRIERS

CULTURE: In Mexico, individuals place great pride in their ability to support their family, particularly related to land ownership — temporary residences or co-ownership faced strong cultural resistance

SCALE REQUIREMENTS: The more buyers that commit to purchasing a house, the cheaper the firm can set the price; however, most solutions are still too expensive for many families to pay in advance

DESIGN LIMITATIONS: At three hundred and twenty square feet, the containers are small — improvements also had to be extremely cost-effective to keep prices down for customers

ENABLERS

STAGED INVESTMENT: The founders won business plan competitions and focused on small amounts of initial funding that lasted until they could convince venture capital investors to jump in

FIND THE WIN-WIN-WIN: PFNC convinced local employers to create methods to spread payment over time by demonstrating that proper housing dramatically increases employee retention and lowers hiring costs

DON'T REINVENT THE WHEEL: PFNC adapted design ideas from small condos and lofts, trailers and jet planes to maximize space utilization and use recycled materials to lower costs

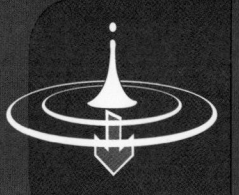

IMPACT

EXTERNAL: PFNC will provide sustainable, affordable housing to some 10,000 families annually in the beginning to transform poor urban areas

COMPETITORS: PFNC is a social venture and it hopes to attract additional players to the market to provide increasingly better housing for the poor

SOCIAL ASPECTS: PFNC Global communities is not only providing housing for the poor, but it also aims to build and develop stable communities in developing regions around the world

WHAT'S NEXT?

PFNC Global Communities is focused on developing its presence in Juarez, Mexico. After proving the business model it hopes to expand to other developing urban areas around the world to increase the number and quality of sustainable urban environments.

Agricultural Sustainability Standards

Standards and certification guidelines to protect rainforest biodiversity at every step in the value chain from producers through consumers

INNOVATION
Standards and certification programs that support companies who engage in sustainable agricultural and economic practices

These firms receive the appropriate recognition and remuneration for their efforts from buyers across the value chain

SUSTAINABILITY
Standards cover environmentally critical issues related to pesticides, deforestation, water and soil protection, and better pay and safe working conditions for farmers

Encourages producers to drive more rapid innovation and uptake of new sustainable practices

RESULTS
Over the last eight years companies like Chiquita (responsible for 25% of North American and European food consumption) have certified all their own farms as well as most of their suppliers' farms, improving environmental and living conditions in communities across Latin America

DRIVERS

TACKLE THE ELEPHANTS: Agriculture is the single largest user of fresh water; moreover, overgrazing, agricultural mismanagement, and deforestation have degraded over four billion acres of land globally

FOUNDERS' PASSION: Founded in 1987, the Rainforest Alliance grew from "the passion of a masseuse, a toxicologist, a theater worker, a returned Peace Corps volunteer, and a young China expert with … no business skills"

DEMAND PULL: News on the impacts of global warming and deforestation increasingly influenced consumers who wanted a way to support sustainable practices, but didn't have a clear line of site to production

BARRIERS

A FEW POWERFUL PRODUCERS: In many crops a few large producers or processors had a great deal of power and seemed immune to pressure and concerns about environmental and social conditions

LOTS OF SMALL FARMS: There is a large number of unorganized family and subsistence farms disconnected from the end market and with limited access to innovative practices and processes

LACK OF STANDARDS: No accepted common standards exist across a wide variety of ecosystems and a wide variety of crops and business models/types

ENABLERS

ENVIRONMENTAL COALITIONS: The Sustainable Agriculture Network, a coalition of environmental groups in eight tropical nations, developed a sustainability auditing process and standards that were able to bridge business and environmental groups

LEAD ADOPTERS: Large companies like Chiquita Brands, as well as cooperatives of smaller farms, led the standards and certification effort, building market advantage and a following including Kraft Foods, Whole Foods, and Mars

NGOs & OTHER COLLABORATIVES: The Alliance has become a hub for a other initiatives and sponsors of rural sustainability advances throughout the tropics

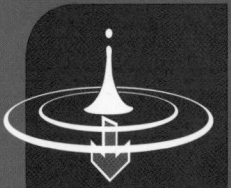

IMPACT

ENVIRONMENTAL CONDITIONS: Over 100 million acres of farmland and forests have adopted the Rainforest Alliance's certification standards and zero deforestation goal, resulting in vastly improved environmental conditions.

INNOVATION & TECH TRANSFER: From new conservation / recycling techniques to new partnerships and value chain relationships and to new processing technologies, the pace of green innovation has increased dramatically

SOCIO-ECONOMIC IMPACT: Rainforest-certified product sales hit $2 billion in 2006, impacting working and living conditions across rural farming communities

WHAT'S NEXT?

Recently celebrating its 20th year, the Rainforest Alliance has continued to increase its impact by about 10% per year. It embraces new innovations and has moved its certification programs into cattle ranching and the sustainable production of soy, palm oil, sugar and biofuel crops.

COMPANIES INNOVATING TO CREATE A MORE SUSTAINABLE WORLD

Zero-Waste On-Demand Packing & Moving

A comprehensive, Zero-Waste packing and moving system developed from 100% recycled trash

INNOVATION
Rentable containers and packing materials made from recycled materials replace traditional cardboard boxes and other packing materials for moving

SUSTAINABILITY
The containers and packaging are made from 100% recycled, post-consumer, end-of-life waste

After 400 uses, each box is recycled to make a new box

RESULTS
By 2010 the company made 138,000 deliveries, eliminating 17,400 tons of trash from landfills, 21,450 tons of new waste, and 104,000 tons in CO_2 emissions while saving 265,000 trees— efforts are now scaling up nationally and internationally

DRIVERS

LEADER'S VISION: Spencer Brown started the company when he saw two stagnant trash piles — his cardboard boxes used for moving and a pile of plastic bottles — and thought of using recycled plastic to re-invent the cardboard box

WASTEFUL STATUS-QUO: Over 20% of the US population packs and moves each year, leading to massive amounts of packing waste that usually ends up in a landfill after just one use

POOR CUSTOMER EXPERIENCE: Managing cardboard boxes and packing materials can be a very frustrating aspect of moving — a significant portion of time is spent simply assembling, breaking down and disposing of the boxes!

BARRIERS

INGRAINED BEHAVIORS: Systems for recycling plastic and for moving were so established that potential recycling partners and customers were not aware there could be an easy and more environmentally friendly solution

LACK OF AVAILABILITY: So far, services are provided in only 12 locations in the US plus Ontario, Canada and Australia

LESS FLEXIBLE ALTERNATIVE: Renting boxes for 2 weeks — the rent-a-green-box policy — forces customers to schedule packing, whereas previously the process could be done more gradually

ENABLERS

GETTING THE WORD OUT: The company's activities are visible through TV shows, online videos, blogs, speaker events, print media and word of mouth, making their efforts to provide sustainable packing materials much more visible

COMMITTED PARTNERS: Partnerships will enable them to serve 43 markets in 10 national locations in 2009 and 2010 and licenses have also been granted for Australia and Canada

CONVENIENT PACKING: The packing materials are delivered directly to the customer with no assembly or tape required — boxes are crush proof, tear proof, weather proof, stable and stackable, enabling moves of all sizes

IMPACT

RECOGNITION: The company has won numerous awards and recognition such as the California Small Business Award in 2009, Entrepreneur of the Month from OC Metro Business and EPA WasteWise Partner in 2008

MOVING COSTS: Using the firm's "Recopack" boxes and the other recyclable packing materials can save customers up to 50% in moving costs and decrease time spent moving

MOVING EXPERIENCE: Customers are thrilled with the company's simplified moving process that provides all the packing materials required and then quickly reclaims them once unpacking is done

WHAT'S NEXT?

The company is currently expanding nationwide through franchising and licensing. They have also invented three more Zero-Waste packing and moving products to pack dishes, glasses and garments

4 Platforms for Sustainable Leadership

An explicit firm-wide focus on Developing Earth-Responsible Raw Materials, Reducing Resource Use, Preventing Insect-Borne Diseases, and Strengthening Communities

INNOVATION
Responsible leadership, new business models and partnerships with the US EPA, other global climate leaders, suppliers and customers to go beyond regulation and industry standards while improving financial performance

SUSTAINABILITY
Driving more use of the most environmentally sustainable in their products and less use of fossil fuels across their value chain

Committed to the Bottom of the Pyramid (BoP) and building sustainable local businesses

RESULTS
Greenhouse gas emissions cut by 27% since 2001 while growing the company

Reducing 61 Million pounds of VOCs from their products while improving their performance

Converting to 36% renewable energy while reducing costs

DRIVERS

TRACK RECORD: Exploring the Amazon for a sustainable source of wax (camauba palm); the first to eliminate CFCs in 1975; one of the first members of Climate Leader Program

INGREDIENT INFO: Consumers are demanding clearer info on product ingredients, origins, purpose, and overall environmental impact

BOTTOM OF PYRAMID: The company saw the potential of a trillion dollar unaddressed market with a huge need for health and sanitation improvements

LEADER'S VISION: Fisk Johnson, like his father and grandfather, has demonstrated and communicated a strong sustainability commitment

BARRIERS

NOT MY PROBLEM: Many companies try to maximize profits while meeting the minimum regulatory requirements

LABEL COMPLEXITY: Household cleaning and personal care products have very complex ingredients; labels are unintelligible to many

AWARENESS + COST: Most BOP customers do not know what is available — and what is available is too expensive or too difficult to obtain

GLOBAL STRUCTURE: Being a global company with a country-based structure along with fragmented market and regulatory structure makes leadership difficult

ENABLERS

FAMILY OWNERSHIP: "Going beyond standards and regulations" is good for business; being family owned enables this $8B firm to make a substantial difference

GREENLIST PROCESS: SCJ developed and vetted a standard process for rating ingredients from acceptable to better to best... then shared the process with industry

BOP PROTOCOLS: SCJ developed protocols and partnerships in developing countries and communities to drive healthy business/community development

COMMITTED PARTNERS: SCJ partnered with the US EPA (e.g. Climate Leaders, Design for Environment, and SmartWay Transport) other nations and suppliers to "green" their supply chain

IMPACT

PUSH THE ENVELOPE: Aggressive absolute targets of greenhouse gas emission reduction (27%) and renewable power now make up 36% of electricity needs

"BEST & BETTER": SCJ has increased use of ingredients in the better and best categories from 36% to 47%; while still improving performance (e.g. Windex and Shout)

BOP POSITIONING: Millions of families received education on diseases from SCJ partnerships; new businesses and co-ops have been created

LEADERSHIP PREMIUM: SCJ's commitment to stay ahead of regulations and standards across the globe has enabled it to take business advantage of powerful green position

WHAT'S NEXT?

The company recently became one of the leading participants in the Green-e Consumer Labeling Program enabling it to further demonstrate to consumers that its products are made in a cleaner way, another example of how SCJ continues to look for new stretch targets to drive itself, its partners, its suppliers and its customers to a more sustainable home and community.

COMPANIES INNOVATING TO CREATE A MORE SUSTAINABLE WORLD

Organic Yogurt with a Message

Combining organic dairy products with a zero carbon footprint claim and an educational mission around sustainable farming and living

INNOVATION
Stonyfield Farms was one of the first to successfully use sustainability leadership and messaging to drive market share and customer loyalty

Stonyfield walks the talk with a powerful customer hand-shake and a sustainability message on every lid

SUSTAINABILITY
Relentlessly driving the sustainability focus and targets across the entire value chain from farm to table and back

Work actively with partners in shipping, packaging, dairy farming, sugar cane plantations, food processing

RESULT
1st US manufacturer certified as carbon neutral (1996)

Environmental sustainability messages and activities on millions of yogurt lids

High growth and profitable company now part of Groupe Danone, enabling a broader impact

DRIVERS

ECONOMIC SELF INTEREST: Early failure of publically funded missionary initiatives convinced CEO that sustainability had to be business led

EDUCATIONAL GOAL: The entire organization and its value chain partners are invested in the educational mission of the company

LEADER'S VISION: CEO has maintained a lifelong commitment to sustainability and a passion for proving that companies can both make money and save the world

BARRIERS

PROFITABILITY QUEST: Prevailing view was that sustainable practices and initiatives were costly and did not pay back

LIMITED AUDIENCE: The speaking circuit has only limited impact and the employee base was small

HIGH COST OF MARKETING: Traditional marketing would have cost tens of millions to get the company enough market share to maintain initial shelf space

SKEPTICISM: Big chains did not believe that niche brands could maintain market share and price premiums

ENABLERS

LEAD BY EXAMPLE: Stonyfield was able to lead by example with their own farms and production facilities and share lessons learned with others on the value chain

PACKAGING AND LIDS: With a large and growing customer base, the company used the packaging and lids as an educational medium

GREEN MARKETING: Distribution, branding and marketing activities focused on segments likely to be interested in addressing environmental challenges

CUSTOMER PROMISE: The power of the promise and the commitment to teach and act has proven the value of staying on message to obtain green objectives

IMPACT

SUSTAINABLE VALUE CHAIN: Able to demonstrate higher profitability and yield with sustainable techniques in both dairy and sugar cane farming

CUSTOMERS: Customers actively read and follow eco-tips that range from how to operate your refrigerator more efficiently to saving the sustainable family farm

10X IMPACT ON SHARE: Campaigns in Chicago and Houston drove initial share to maintain shelf space and then build loyalty with high quality and green positioning

EASE OF ENTRY: Sustainability has become a powerful platform to allow Stonyfield to enter new markets as a powerful member of the Groupe Danone family

WHAT'S NEXT?

Stonyfileld has grown by an average of 27% per year for the past eighteen straight years compared to 5-7% for its industry. The intent is to move to 100% sustainable packaging by 2015 (minimal, recyclable, biodegradable) and to significantly influence other food and consumer products companies in the process.

Turn the Trash into Cash

There is no such thing as waste for TerraCycle, a company that uses garbage as raw material for its entire product line

INNOVATION
Using the insight that people are willing to pay a premium to help dispose of their garbage, Terra-Cycle built its for-profit business model on manufacturing products out of waste

SUSTAINABILITY
Reusing waste as raw material reduces both the amount of virgin materials needed for manufacturing as well as the resources ending up in landfills

RESULTS
TerraCycle doubles its revenues every year and is expected to hit $15 million in 2009

The company offers more than 50 different products in the US, UK, Mexico, and Brazil

DRIVERS

FINANCIAL TIPPING POINT: Skyrocketing landfill costs and improving recycling technologies suggest a growing opportunity in garbage management

CLIMATE CHANGE: Changes in the weather are already noticeable, alerting customers and quick-moving companies to the value of reusing natural resources

LEADER'S VISION: While studying at Princeton, founder Tom Szaky saw that the garbage business will be the next big thing and decided in 2001 to drop out to found his own company — he has managed it ever since

BARRIERS

RAW MATERIAL SUPPLY: TerraCycle had difficulty finding a legal and financially viable sourcing model — its initial goal to take the initiative to collect waste materials from neighborhood garbage sites turned out to be illegal

NO SACRIFICE: Although consumers regard environmental issues as very important, they resist raising prices and sacrificing performance in order to make a particular product greener

INITIAL FUNDING: Due to a dispute about the company's business plan, the founders refused $1M in initial funding from investors — this threatened the company's viability as they couldn't buy packaging for the first products

ENABLERS

INVOLVE ALL STAKEHOLDERS: Green-minded communities send their waste to TerraCycle or drop it off at partner stores, providing low cost raw materials — the collection programs are also sponsored by product manufacturers

NICHE MARKET: Using the discharge of worm-fed organic waste created a competitively priced, premium product that could serve as the first product line of the company without requiring a large initial investment

RECYCLED PACKAGING: Making both the product and the package from garbage (e.g., empty soda bottles & misprinted cardboard boxes) lowered production costs

IMPACT

PARTNER COMPANIES: Innovative reuse of non-recyclable garbage motivated major original manufacturers — Capri Sun, Frito-Lay, Kraft, Wrigley — to partner with TerrraCycle

EXTERNAL: TerraCycle's 50+ products are being sold in major stores in North America — revenues are doubling annually and the products and ideas from the company attract continuous media coverage

COMPETITORS: TerraCycle has the first-mover advantage in the mass production of garbage-based products — garbage suppliers partner with TerraCycle to enter this market

WHAT'S NEXT?

TerraCycle is currently expanding its operations to the UK, Mexico and Brazil. Eventually, the company aspires to be the Procter & Gamble of garbage, aiming to eliminate even the idea of waste by reusing everything possible.

COMPANIES INNOVATING TO CREATE A MORE SUSTAINABLE WORLD

Eco-Environment

Building an Eco-Friendly Environment One Store at a Time

INNOVATION

An ecologically friendly retail environment created from new low-carbon technology, sustainable consumer products and eco-friendly superstores all aiming to reduce carbon emissions and Tesco's global footprint

SUSTAINABILITY

Technology that reduces operating costs, carbon emissions and energy consumption

Higher sales of sustainable products

Reduced carbon footprint from superstores

RESULTS

An overall 70% carbon footprint reduction in Tesco pilot stores

New low-carbon technologies that are ready to be used across all Tesco global superstores

Greater customer loyalty

DRIVERS

CUT MY COSTS: With energy costs on the rise, Tesco sought bottom line savings through the development of technologies to reduce energy consumption by 48% from baseline measures in 2006

THE GOOD NEIGHBOR: Building customer trust and loyalty by offering a healthier shopping experience and more sustainable products

STAKING THEIR REPUTATION: The CEO publically stated in 2007 that Tesco would reduce carbon emissions at least 50% by 2020 and develop a new model of operational sustainability

BARRIERS

LACK OF TECHNOLOGY: Although new low-carbon technologies continue to emerge, only a small percentage of these inventions have been tested, certified for use, or proven to be economically viable

CUSTOMER ADOPTION: Customers were in support of products to reduce carbon emissions, but the costs were high and customers did not understand how they could make a difference — lack of proper incentive systems

HIGH COSTS: The costs of designing a fully sustainable superstore were very high, and there were no success stories from other stores to determine the viability of an eco-friendly retail environment

ENABLERS

PRIVATE INVESTMENT: Tesco took the initiative to create a €100 million fund that would support the development and use of new low-carbon technology — products would be tested in Tesco pilot stores

NEW INITIATIVES: Initiatives include: increasing information for consumers; displaying carbon cost of products; a green clubcard to reward customers for re-using plastic bags; and making sustainable products affordable

NEW STORE MODEL: With the CEO's new vision for a sustainable future, Tesco created a blueprint to design a pilot store to demonstrate effective carbon emission reductions

IMPACT

NEW CAPABILITIES: Pilot stores allowed Tesco to incorporate new technologies that led to the creation of the new "Eco Store" that maximizes natural light, ventilation, rainwater and renewable energy on site

GROWING CUSTOMER LOYALTY: Customers are more willing to purchase products and support initiatives that have a positive impact on the environment — a more loyal customer base

SUSTAINABLE FUTURE: With the successful launch of the pilot store, Tesco has now extended this blueprint to other stores in other countries to achieve the 70% reduction in carbon footprint done in Tesco pilot Eco Store

WHAT'S NEXT?

With the successful reduction in carbon emissions and the creation of a more energy efficient Eco Store, Tesco aims to apply these new technologies to existing and new Tesco Stores.

High Performance Electric Sports Car

Sports car buyers are less concerned about price and range limits of current e-vehicles — expand to broader segments as technologies improve

INNOVATION
High performance electric vehicles (EVs) that can seat two passengers and are capable of going from 0-60 mph in 3.9 seconds

Vehicles can fully charge in less than 4 hours using a standard 110V or 220V outlet

SUSTAINABILITY
For a 300 mile drive, the cost of power consumed by the E-roadster is equivalent to 10% the cost of driving a regular vehicle 300 miles

The vehicle can be powered from 100% renewable energy sources

RESULTS
The E-roadster, with an efficiency equivalent to any high end sports car, can drive up to 244 miles with a full charge that costs $5

Advertising Age named Tesla one of the 50 hottest brands

DRIVERS

HIGH GASOLINE PRICES: Sustained gasoline prices of $3-4 per gallon are making EVs much more cost competitive at about 1/10 the annual operating cost of gas-powered vehicles

LEADER'S PASSION: Elon Musk and his team at Tesla Motors have exhibited a strong and sustained passion for clean energy and electric vehicles

GOVERNMENT INCENTIVES: There are now significant government incentives for all electric vehicles, including about $5,000 on a $50,000 electric sedan

BARRIERS

BATTERY SIZE AND COST: Rechargeable lithium batteries are still very costly and take up a lot of space

LOW PRODUCTION VOLUMES: A $100,000 roadster and a $50,000 sedan will still only support relatively low production volumes of 15,000 to 20,000 a year at California plant

POOR MARKET PERCEPTION: Wide publicity of 300 mile range and acceleration from 0-60 in 5.5 seconds for 5-7 passenger sedan still hasn't dented public perception of performance limits

ENABLERS

IMPROVED CHARGING: Lower cost and easier charging options combined with lithium ion battery technology improvements increase single charge range to 300 miles

SIMPLER ENGINE AND DRIVE: Far simpler engine and drive components with fewer moving parts lowers production costs even for small volume production

MORE CHARGING OPTIONS: An increased availability of charging and switching stations combined with the ease of charging at home and during off-peak periods make charging far less difficult

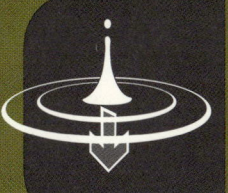

IMPACT

INDUSTRY: Tesla Motors has become one of the most successful automotive startups and its $109,000 model has been in production for two years — partnering with Daimler, it is blazing an EV path in the upper market segments

SUPPLIERS: Electronics and battery suppliers have become more aggressive now that Tesla has demonstrated the production market for all electric vehicles — Tesla is also partnering to build out charging station networks

CUSTOMERS: Although primarily a show car at present, the dealer network is expanding internationally and high profile owners like the governor of California are helping create even more buzz

WHAT'S NEXT?

Tesla Motors unveiled its second all-electric car, a seven passenger $50,000 (after tax credits) high performance sedan that will be available in late 2011. Factoring in operating costs, the true costs of this EV will be roughly equivalent to a $35,000 gas-powered sedan.

COMPANIES INNOVATING TO CREATE A MORE SUSTAINABLE WORLD

Prius Gas-Electric Hybrid

Use less gas through a hybrid technology solution combined with real-time driver feedback that is simple and makes sense

INNOVATION
Fuel economy goals for the Prius drove engineers to develop an entirely new automobile

Developed control system that optimizes gas and electric engine usage

Real-time display to inform and involve drivers on how best to drive the car

SUSTAINABILITY
Gets twice the mileage compared to similar-size non-hybrid cars

Captures kinetic energy into electrical energy when braking

Significantly reduced emissions of CO_2 and NO_2

RESULT
Since 1996, over 1.7 million Toyota hybrids have been sold leading to a reduction of ~9M tons of CO_2

DRIVERS

THE BIG AUDACIOUS GOAL: Since the project conception, Toyota's leaders pushed the firm to build a car that was 100% more fuel efficient — engineers were forced to look beyond traditional internal combustion engine

TACKLE THE ELEPHANT: The company recognized its large and growing contribution to emissions and fuel consumption and sought ways to reduce its impact

PENDING REGULATIONS: Despite skepticism about US market potential, increasingly stringent vehicle emissions laws in California convinced Toyota's leaders that revolutionary fuel mileage would be critical in the future

BARRIERS

FAST FOLLOWERS: Toyota was historically a very risk-averse company extremely focused on process efficiency over product or technology innovation

FEW TECHNOLOGIES: At the time, there were little or no commercially available technologies required to build a car that could switch between electric and gas power sources

WHERE'S THE MARKET?: Toyota wanted the Prius to be a key growth platform for the US market; however, in the late 1990's many potential customers were still wedded to large, high capacity, SUVs

ENABLERS

SENIOR SUPPORT: Most companies targeted making a 100% electric car while Toyota recognized that the hybrid was attractive enough and more actionable — Toyota leaders saw importance of Prius and supported it

ALL HANDS ON DECK: Toyota used more than 1,000 engineers to research, develop and produce the Prius in less than 24 months — 30% faster that the company usually took for new car development

RED CARPET TREATMENT: Combined with spikes in gasoline prices and greater environmental awareness, a number of high profile celebrities purchased, drove and spread the word that hybrids, not SUVs, were cool

IMPACT

INTERNAL: By proving the company was capable of this unusually innovative project, Toyota's culture has been significantly altered to support the company's new leadership position in hybrids and beyond

COMPETITORS: The Prius proved that a mass-production hybrid was a solid and attractive business leading to similar hybrid car development projects across every major car maker in the world

CUSTOMERS: Building on the growing automobile sustainability trend, the Prius changed customer perceptions of hybrids from a novelty to a symbol of global responsibility

WHAT'S NEXT?

Toyota continues to set ambitions goals including an internal target of 1 million hybrid sales by the early 2010s achieved through the launch of as many as 10 new hybrid models globally; furthermore, Toyota plans to offer a hybrid power train for every model in the 2020s.

The Gold Standard for Green Building

Drive sustainable building design, construction and operation through a sensible, consensus-based certification system

INNOVATION

An open and transparent rating and certification system that aligns the varied interests of architects, builders, owners and operators to support and encourage environmentally sustainable construction across a building's lifecycle

A certification system that professionals want and that developers want for their buildings

SUSTAINABILITY

Rating system makes impact measurable in key areas like building and site design, water efficiency, energy use, materials and resource types, and indoor environmental quality

A universally accepted standard that stakeholders can value and price — creating long term rewards for those who meet minimum criteria

RESULT

Buildings that are LEED certified in the US save 25-30% on energy and 7% on water compared to those that are not certified — resulting in substantial reductions in CO_2 emissions

In 2009, LEED projects were already on their way in more than 40 countries

DRIVERS

GOVERNMENT INITIATIVES: The private sector and NGOs wanted a way to collaborate with the US government to standardize sustainability targets for buildings and create the right set of incentives for all stakeholders

CUSTOMER PULL: Organizations were increasingly interested in renting eco-friendly buildings due to environmental, health, and financial reasons, but had no means to reliably quantify the benefits of different buildings

TECHNOLOGY PUSH: Companies producing more sustainable building materials needed an independent authority to validate the true benefits and environmental impact of their products for potential buyers

BARRIERS

COST OF COMPLIANCE: High cost of sustainable design and construction — from researching new approaches to procuring proper materials — made investors uncertain about the overall return on their investment

SKEWED SYSTEM: Original ratings sometimes incentivized environmentally poor choices, such as encouraging fossil fuel use, because the system failed to account for regional differences, like materials supply and climate

LACK OF KNOWLEDGE: Many builders did not have experience working on sustainable construction and development projects — the increased delays and higher costs to go green deterred these critical stakeholders

ENABLERS

GOVERNMENT INCENTIVES: To increase LEED adoption, local governments provided incentive programs that included tax credits and breaks, free or reduced fees and grants or low interest loans for LEED certified buildings

QUICK ADAPTATION: LEED was designed to be continuously updated to address the criticism that it can't be used everywhere or is biased — the 2009 version has already been adjusted to tackle many regional issues

CHAMPION: Robert K. Watson, a recognized pioneer of the modern green building movement, used his global experience and credibility to spearhead the development of LEED

IMPACT

ACROSS THE VALUE CHAIN: LEED certified real estate translates into higher rent premiums, higher occupancy rates and lower building operating costs which is creating further demand for certification

SOCIETY: Many government and private institutions across the US now use the LEED certification system as the major standard for specifying sustainable construction guidelines

INDUSTRY: In the latest version of the certification, a set of sustainable building and management best practices are being collected and synthesized to increase knowledge transfer and building performance

WHAT'S NEXT?

Common standards create a platform for rapid innovation — builders and buildings now tout their LEED (Leadership in Energy and Environmental Design) credentials as a bragging right and key selling point.

Microloans for Local Farmers

Low-interest loans offered to small, local producers to help grow their businesses and increase the supply of organic food for consumers

INNOVATION

Program offers $10 million annually for local farmers to expand their business and bring more local and organic products to market

Faster and cheaper than traditional financing options like banks

SUSTAINABILITY

Supports organic and animal compassionate producers who meet Whole Foods' quality and animal welfare standards

Locally produced foods have substantially lower carbon footprints

RESULTS

In the two years since the program started, Whole Foods has given out $2.5 million in loans to 41 people in 18 states

The average amount given out for loans is $52,292

DRIVERS

SAME MODEL, NEW REGION: Inspired by the success of their non-profit arm in offering microloans to producers in developing countries, Whole Foods launched a similar program for local US producers

DEMAND PULL: In recent years, there has been increasing demand for local produce as consumers believe it is fresher and tastes better than produce grown in distant locations

COSTS AND RED TAPE: Local producers who want to expand their businesses have a low probability of getting loans from traditional banks — even when they do, the processing is tedious, takes a long time and the costs are high

BARRIERS

LOAN SIZE: The targeted loan amounts, which are between $1,000 and $100,000 with a maximum $25,000 for startups, may not be enough for some producers aiming for larger expansions into Whole Food stores

INTERNAL PROCESSES: Whole Foods switched to a regional distribution system to improve supply chain efficiency; however, the switch made it difficult for local producers to sell their products directly to Whole Foods stores

ESTABLISHED SYSTEMS: The industrialization and consolidation of food production has caused many local (i.e., often smaller) farmers to exit the industry — finding enough local producers for each store was a challenge

ENABLERS

ADDITIONAL FINANCING: Local producers looking to expand their businesses further are given the opportunity to apply for additional financing in the same program after one year if the initial loan is in good financial standing

PERSONAL RELATIONSHIPS: The company assigns a person to each supplier to establish a relationship, become familiar with the supplier's business and products and act as the point of contact for loans and sales

CHEAPER AND FASTER: Whole Foods set up the loan program to offer a more streamlined process with one fee, minimal paperwork and a less expensive option with low fixed interest rates of 5% - 9%

IMPACT

HALO EFFECT: Support from Whole Foods through the loan program increases the standing of suppliers and allows them to secure financing from traditional banks

CUSTOMERS: Many loan recipients have been featured by newspapers and TV shows, increasing customer awareness of Whole Foods' commitment to local food production

COMPANY OFFERING: The program has helped a diverse group of suppliers, expanding products such as ice cream, organic produce, wine sorbet, grass-fed beef and raw gluten-free granola

WHAT'S NEXT?

Whole Foods looks to continue providing loans to local producers with 20 more applications in the pipeline as of late 2009.

Car Sharing for City Dwellers

Reduce the number of cars in cities through an always available car service customized for the transportation needs of individuals in cities

INNOVATION

Zipcar's car-as-a-service offers cars and trucks in specific urban areas for short periods of time — as little as thirty minutes

Rental fee includes all maintenance and gas costs for a convenient and reliable service

SUSTAINABILITY

Zipcars enable city dwellers to share cars, increasing utilization of each vehicle

Members plan and combine multiple auto trips into one, reducing fuel consumption and emissions

RESULTS

Zipcar is the world's largest car sharing service proving the cars-as-a-service model

Over 2 million people live within a five-minute walk of a Zipcar

As a result, 50,000 cars have been taken off the road

DRIVERS

EMPTY SEATS: People only drive their cars a fraction of the overall time they own them — in an urban environment, the supply of unused cars far exceeds the demand

COSTS OF OWNERSHIP: Owners must endure high fixed costs to buy, maintain and insure a vehicle — car sharing could distribute these costs

FEW ALTERNATIVES: Public transport does not provide the same level of convenience as private cars while regular car rentals are pricey and often inconveniently located

GREEN CAN BE GOLD: Founder Robin Chase heard about car-sharing in Europe and believed that it could be very profitable while providing social and environmental benefits

BARRIERS

SCALE + LOGISTICS: Matching customers to Zipcars on a profitable scale would have to be automated, but no effective solutions existed

SHARING IS SCARY: People can be wary of sharing, particularly personal items like cars, a notion confirmed during initial brand testing that revealed strong negative reactions to the word "sharing"

LACK OF EXPERIENCE: On a mission to change the world, the founder expanded rapidly, but exceeded the ability of the firm to manage its resources well — investors forced the founder out and pulled funding

ENABLERS

TECHNOLOGY: Zipcar developed proprietary online vehicle reservation and card ID systems that enable members to quickly locate, reserve and access Zipcars and the company to monitor and improve service

IT'S HIP TO ZIP: Lime green cars, member networking events and strong community links created a devoted group of "Zipsters" that spread the word to friends, family and the community

PILOT AND GROW: A new CEO with experience growing startups shifted Zipcar's efforts to densely populated areas and refocused the mission on efficient growth to ensure the firm could generate long-term financial and social impact

IMPACT

INDUSTRY: The success of a cars-as-a-service business model has created a new industry that has spurred start-ups and existing rental-car agencies to roll-out competing offers

CUSTOMERS: Evidence suggests that Zipcar users are changing their driving behavior in environmentally beneficial ways including reduced and more efficient driving and increased use of public transport

INTERNAL: A refocused Zipcar attracted over $40 million from investors to support the company's expansion to over 50 locations — the company expects to be profitable in 2009

WHAT'S NEXT?

Zipcar will continue to grow in urban environments as the company works towards its goal to have car-sharing members outnumber individual car owners in major cities worldwide. The firm is also expanding into different markets that could potentially support a small fleet of Zipcars — for example, to universities across the US.

AUTHORS

Hitendra Patel, Ph.D.
Founder & Managing Director, IXL Center, Professor of Innovation and Growth at Hult IBS

Hitendra is the Founder and Managing Director of IXL Center & Chair of the Innovation and Growth Program at the Hult International Business School. Hitendra was a senior leader and co-founder of Monitor Group's Innovation Practice and was responsible for Asia and Latin America. Prior to Monitor, he was a senior manager at Arthur D. Little. As a management consultant, he has made lasting impact with all types of companies by helping them identify new engines for growth and develop their own capacity to innovate. Hitendra has also helped and published articles at the national and region level on the topic of economic development in Brazil, India, Indonesia, Singapore, the US and the UK.

Ronald S. Jonash
Director & Senior Partner, IXL Center, Professor of Innovation and Growth at Hult IBS

Ron is a Senior Partner at IXL Center and at Spinnaker Group (a venture capital firm). He is on the faculty of the Hult International Business School and on the Advisory board of Arthur D. Little Inc. (ADL). He was most recently a senior partner of the Monitor Group where he founded and led their Innovation practice and was founder of IMI (Innovation Management Inc.). For 20 years he was the managing director of the Technology and Innovation Management Practice for Arthur D. Little worldwide. He was also Chief Innovation Officer and served on their Technology Investment Board and Management Education Institute Board.

Tyler McNally
Associate Director & Partner, IXL Center

Tyler is an Associate Director and Partner at IXL Center. He is responsible for project integration, advisory, and client management. In addition, he is an instructor and facilitator of IXL's Innovation and Growth courses and workshops. Tyler is also a major contributor to IXL's innovation content, including innovation research, articles, white papers, and curriculum. Prior to IXL, Tyler was a case team leader for the Monitor Group, managing projects in the US, UAE, Saudi Arabia and Iraq. He has worked with the public and private sector on a range of issues related to national economic development, innovation management, corporate strategy and finance, and new product development and commercialization.

Mark Rennella, Ph.D.
Principal

Mark earned a Ph.D. in American history in 2001 and has researched and published extensively on the cultural and business implications of international travel. After having taught at Harvard's History and Literature Program from 1997 to 2003, he finished major projects on the topics of marketing and leadership as a Research Associate at Harvard Business School. His most recent publication, Entrepreneurs, Managers, and Leaders: What the Airline Industry Can Teach Us about Leadership (Palgrave Macmillan, 2009), offers a history of the US airlines that investigates the relationship between leadership and industry evolution.

CONTRIBUTORS

Julius Bautista
Consultant

Kyle Baizas
Analyst

Joanna Chua
Consultant

Samuel Freeman
Principal, IXL Canada

Dr. Milagros Masini
Principal, IXL Center

Milena Koleva
Analyst

Venkateswaran Kumar
Analyst

Szabolcs Patay
Analyst

Prakash Rajasekharan
Analyst

Endre A. Sagi
Analyst

Pradyum Sekar
Principal, IXL Canada

GREENOVATIONS AT A GLANCE

GREENOVATIONS BY GEOGRAPHY

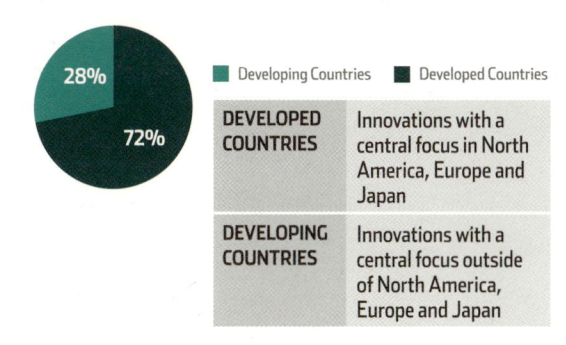

- Developing Countries: 28%
- Developed Countries: 72%

DEVELOPED COUNTRIES	Innovations with a central focus in North America, Europe and Japan
DEVELOPING COUNTRIES	Innovations with a central focus outside of North America, Europe and Japan

GREENOVATIONS BY THEME

- Efficiency: 54%
- Renewable/Natural Resources: 24%
- Waste Management & Recycling: 22%

EFFICIENCY	Producing more for less (e.g. cost reduction)
RENEWABLE /NATURAL RESOURCES	Utilizing renewable or natural resources to produce energy and products such as plastics and food
WASTE MANAGEMENT & RECYCLING	Finding ways to reduce or reuse waste

GREENOVATIONS BY INDUSTRY

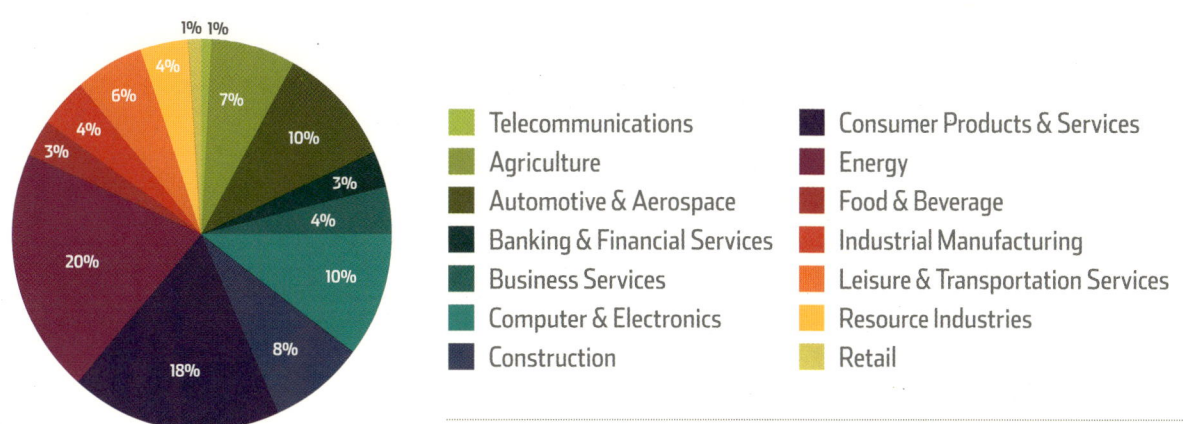

- Telecommunications: 1%
- Agriculture: 1%
- Automotive & Aerospace: 7%
- Banking & Financial Services: 10%
- Business Services: 3%
- Computer & Electronics: 4%
- Construction: 10%
- Consumer Products & Services: 8%
- Energy: 18%
- Food & Beverage: 20%
- Industrial Manufacturing: 3%
- Leisure & Transportation Services: 4%
- Resource Industries: 6%
- Retail: 4%

Note: Greenovations may be counted in more than one industry depending on their nature

IXL Center would like to thank the 2009 MBA candidates from the Boston Campus of the Hult International Business School for providing valuable research that supported the development of this book.

2009 HULT CLASS

- Rania Abd El-Salam
- Astha Agarwal
- Aina Anibaba
- Douglas Araujo
- Chyabhorn Athaweth-Worawuth
- Eno Atoyebi
- Anjul Bahuguna
- Carlo Enrique Baizas
- Sandeep Balagangadharan
- Gianluigi Barletta
- Neli Batista
- Cristiano Caetano Da Cruz
- Aimin Cao
- Dilip Chatulingath
- Wan-Hsun Chiu
- Tze Fang Chong
- Caroline Costa
- Andre De Carvalho
- Maarten De Laet
- Ricardo dos Santos
- Rea Erne Kauer
- Guillermo Escarraga
- Melissa Espinoza Rincon
- Claire Fang
- Alejandro Fernandez Montes
- Daniel Frech
- Dmitry Gamayunov
- Yvonne Garcelon
- Ivo Gasulla
- Sudarshan Ghimire
- Miguel Goncalves
- Cornelia Grafin von Westarp
- Ixchel Guerrero Castillo
- Kathia Guerrero Ramirez
- Rahul Gupta
- Divyan Gupta
- Sunil Gupta
- Elise Haerle
- Masahiro Hamade
- Osamu Hara
- Javier Heighes
- Jessica Hein
- Hector Hinostroza Acuna
- Alexandra Hodgson
- Theodoros Ioannidis
- Irina Ivanova
- Dheeraj Jalali
- Rakshit Joshi
- Martin Kauer
- Finan Khim
- Jung Sik Kim
- Meranie Kiwanuka
- Milena Koleva
- Eugen Krasowski
- Dimitris Krikis
- Manoj Kudilingal
- Mrinal Kumar
- Venkateswaran Kumar
- Mamiko Kuno
- Jorge Lepervanche
- Victor Lescano
- Chi-San Lo
- Keshav Loomba
- Mariya Loshkevich
- Rodrigo Magboo
- Ernesto Manaure
- Paula Martinez
- Diego Mendes
- Subrat Mohanty
- Sinora Mordecai
- Mark Morgan
- Raghunath Nadiger
- Walid Nakad
- Preethi Narayan
- Carlos Nouel
- Wei Tak Nyou
- Ikenna Okechukwu
- Dianne Oliphant
- Roque Glenn Omanio
- Diego Orozco
- Sherif Osman
- Aristeidis Papathanos
- Christian Peric
- Francesca Pizzuti
- Sathish Raju
- Shashi Ranjan
- Rohit Rathi
- Leonardo Ratti
- Arjun Rawat
- Paolo Reggio d'Aci
- Jaime Rincon
- Rodrigo Robles
- Erika Robles Acero
- Dmitry Rodionov
- Unver Sahin
- Maria Camila Sarmiento Salazar
- Pradyum Sekar
- Paras Sharma
- Sameer Sharma
- Shishir Shetty
- Saki Shigemori
- Yoichi Shono
- Anton Slepenko
- Santiago Suarez
- Yukiko Teshima
- Darsan Thampi
- Junya Tomoi
- Satyavrat Tripathi
- Andrea Uribe
- Haritha Vaddadi
- Laura Mariana Vega Silva
- Sribabu Venkatapathy
- Joao Vilaca
- Edgar Villagomez
- Jaime Villegas
- Rafael Vizcarra Carrasco
- Lindong Wang
- Shunxi Wang
- Erina Watanabe
- Teresa Wu
- Zhongping Xu
- Masayuki Yamada
- Madhu Yeramalli Subraman
- Atsushi Yoneda
- Fredrick Yoon
- Artem Yudin
- Luca Zapparoli
- Carolina Zapponi
- Wei Zhang
- Min Zhu
- Yangcan Zou

Photo Credits: www.flickr.com/photos/neilbetter, www.flickr.com/photos/erikcharlton, www.flickr.com/photos/adventurespf, www.flickr.com/photos/epioles, www.flickr.com/photos/peterpearson, www.flickr.com/photos/viriyincy, www.flickr.com/photos/thessaly, www.flickr.com/photos/lrargerich, www.flickr.com/photos/insmu74, www.flickr.com/photos/hdptcar, www.flickr.com/photos/maskedmalayan, www.flickr.com/photos/alexao, www.flickr.com/photos/dnorman, www.flickr.com/photos/sidelife, www.flickr.com/photos/bensutherland, www.flickr.com/photos/luc, www.flickr.com/photos/stephenliveshere, www.flickr.com/photos/lhoon, www.flickr.com/photos/greeblie, www.flickr.com/photos/ricephotos, www.flickr.com/photos/olpc, www.flickr.com/photos/msvg, www.flickr.com/photos/robinh00d, www.flickr.com/photos/richardwest, www.flickr.com/photos/koffein, www.flickr.com/photos/jurvetson, www.flickr.com/photos/beigephotos, www.flickr.com/photos/claudiacastro, www.flickr.com/photos/seenful, http://www.flickr.com/photos/topgold

A NOTE ON SOURCES

This book is meant to stimulate awareness and discussion around the topics of Sustainability and Innovation.

Factual information in this book including, but not limited to, names, dates, events, financial information and other numerical data were collected from third party publicly available sources. These sources include publications: The Economist, The New York Times, The New Yorker, The Wall Street Journal, and others; sustainability related blogs and websites, government and non-government organizations, company websites and annual reports and others. Where possible, IXL Center also directly contacted the company to corroborate information from public sources.

Other information including analysis, predictions, and assumptions were developed by IXL Center and may not represent the views of the specific companies or representatives from those companies.

For any questions, please contact IXL Center.

Copyright © 2010, IXL Center. All rights reserved. No part of this publication may be reproduced or distributed in any form or by any means, or stored in a database or retrieval system, without the prior written consent of IXL Center, including, but not limited to, in any network or other electronic storage or transmission, or broadcast for distance learning.